You know...

SHE KNOWS

You know...

SHE KNOWS

Secrets to Looking Hot, Being Seductive, and Feeling Sexy

by @queen.vee.bee

Table of Contents

Preface

I don't reserve my admiration for a woman simply graced with a button nose, a cute face, or naturally long, thick hair—as if she's won the genetic lottery.

What truly captivates me is a woman who knows exactly who she is and has sharpened her unique techniques to a magnetic allure. She's deeply in tune with her body and mind, understanding what accentuates her distinctiveness. She perfected a signature look that is nothing short of artistry.

Like a walking painting, she commands attention—not merely because she's attractive, but because there's something irresistibly special in the way she presents herself. Fully conscious of her beauty, she exudes a self-assured strength that's impossible to ignore.

Her every movement, down to the strategic placement of her hair, is a conscious act. In her presence, it's evident that she not only owns her look but quite simply- **You Know…She Knows**.

Your desire to tune in to your feminine "Guns" is my motivation, and this book is a tribute to our journey together. So, if it is your choice, to become, the hottest version of yourself, here's to our shared passion. Together we will do it.

About Me

Hello there, my Gorgeous reader!

It's me, Queen Vee Bee – You might know me from TikTok, that's where I find myself immersed in my current role as a content creator. I have built an empowering platform where all the girls' girls unite. And the best thing about my "Hot Girl Community?" We always have each other's backs— whether it's hunting down the perfect bra or discovering a to-die-for white blouse. I am amazed by my strong female following, and I simply love connecting with you all through the power of social media. And now it's the right time for me to take it to a book format, so I can reach more stunning females around the world.

For those who don't know me, I am covering a specific niche, that shows women how to be as I like to call it – "Effective Looking." Effective means that it gives the feeling of arousal when people look at YOU. The knowledge I share is through outfit combinations, flirtatious movements, and **Red-Hot Charisma** tips.

You might wonder how I ended up with such a specialized body of knowledge. The answer lies in the path my life has taken, which I believe has naturally led me to accumulate this wisdom. I maintain an expansive mental archive, much like a computer filled with assorted folders of knowledge. Each file has a memory attached to it.

From my teenage years, I've been equipped with a somewhat intuitive knack for discerning what's attractive in a sexy way and what's not - a type of sixth sense, you could say. This could be traced back to my younger days when I was amazed by femineity and the power it can hold. Engrossed in imaginative games of dress-up, I would often echo the iconic lines of renowned film beauties, enamored by their power and charisma. I was particularly drawn to films where women assumed dangerously seductive roles, commanding the narrative with them being in control. One of my ultimate favorites - the telenovela Rubi and old classic, - basic Instinct movie, where Sharon Stone had the iconic leg cross scene. Observing femininity in its dangerously **hot** form has always been a source of awe and delight for me.

Later, fortune graced me with a posse of stunning female friends, each a dazzling gem who revealed valuable allure secrets to me. These beauties continually inspired me to up my game, each bringing their unique beauty hacks to our collective. It was as if I was constructing a mental library brimming with tried-and-tested beauty strategies; that we ventured out to put everything to the test, whether it was a club or dates. Our social engagements were a vibrant testing ground for these ideas.

Let me assure you, this mental library doesn't catalog passing trends or popular styles; it's more of a treasure trove of everlasting **hotness** tips, timeless color and outfit combinations, and even the secrets to charming flirtation and seductive movements.

Another key contributor to my knowledge is my modeling career where I repetitively had to share my living space. Can

You imagine living with seven other striking women in the same apartment? It is an epicenter of a beauty think-tank. Not only did I gain invaluable insights from these women, but also from the perspectives of photographers and the wider fashion industry.

My academic pursuits further nurtured this passion. My bachelor's degree in psychology, continually fuels my intellectual curiosity, propelling me to unravel the complexities and motivations behind the art of attraction. Following that, a fashion school in Dubai provided a privileged glimpse into the beauty of creating and styling garments.

My experiences living in diverse locales have played a significant role too. Born in Latvia, I've been fortunate to live in remarkable cities and countries such as Shanghai in China, Milan in Italy, Ibiza, Mallorca, Marbella in Spain, Dusseldorf in Germany, and the lively city of Dubai where I'm residing for now. These places have exposed me to a wide array of feminine beauty that our world has to offer.

To this day whenever I find myself surrounded by alluring, stunning women, whether it's at a busy bar or a sandy beach, I can't help but notice that some women have a certain sparkle that radiates from deep within them. Exuding purely magical aura, one that steals the spotlight and has all eyes glued to them. They are simply…Irresistible. And I couldn't help but find myself wondering, what is their "Je Ne Sais Quoi[1]."

---

[1] Je Ne Sais Quoi: A French phrase translated as "I don't know what," used to describe an indescribable quality, an elusive and often charming characteristic or attribute that's hard to put into words.

About the Book

Your enchanting recipe book for sizzling allure.

Gorgeous, welcome to your guidebook for **Red-Hot Charisma**!

Let's start with a pressing question for you: Don't you ever grow weary of receiving the same stale, repetitive advice every time you search for ways to look **hot**? The typical advice is always the same— "Be Confident." But you're probably seeking tangible, practical methods, right? Well, that's where this book comes in. It's here to provide you with concrete strategies, each of which has been personally tested and approved based on my own experiences.

Imagine holding a magic wand that can sprinkle you with the perfect dash of allure. This book? It's that wand. Whether you're aiming to dazzle someone special or simply basking in the power of your own magnetism, this book is your sparkling potion.

You know that post-hairdresser glow? That I-can-conquer-the-world kind of vibe with every hair flip? Dive into these pages and discover countless ways to feel that confidence surge over and over.

It's not just about turning heads (though that's a delightful bonus); it's about taking your looks into your own hands and revealing the magic within, letting them be the mirror of your fantasies.

From daily charm to late-night dates, find a treasure trove of insights tailored just for you. Think of this book as your glam fairy godmother, with chapters brimming with combinations and techniques that can elevate your allure. It's the hot best friend, the wise older sister, and the super-femme mother who always has a suggestion up her sleeve, all wrapped up into one.

This book will demonstrate you how to cultivate allure through various elements, including emphasizing your distinct features, mastering the art of movement, taking advantage of scent, the skill of flirtation, fabric choices, clothing combinations, makeup choices, feeling sexy rituals, and a variety of hacks and tricks.

Place it on your nightstand, let it nestle among your makeup brushes, or tuck it inside your closet. Whenever you need a sprinkle of sassy charm, this book is right here, rooting for you, celebrating every stunning version of you.

Your First Pot of Hot Knowledge

In the following pages, you will find techniques and tricks to enhance your beauty. I have discovered that these things work really well.

The "Mannequin Beauty" and "Floating Beauty" Theory

#Accenting-symmetric/asymmetric-face

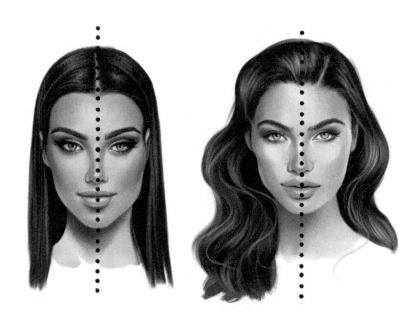

Memory Lane:

The Day of Epiphany: So, there I was, sipping on my latte and investigating my face in a Zoom mirror, singing the "I'm Just a Girl" song. It made me have a fixating moment that my face is not entirely symmetrical. Naturally, I found myself looking at other gorgeous women that day, discovering that many breathtakingly beautiful women indeed possess asymmetrical faces. I wondered, Could there be a way to enhance this particular trait?

Journey Into Inquisition: This curiosity sparked an extensive research phase. I classified women based on the symmetry and the asymmetry in their facial features, identifying the most impressive examples of both. In my quest to understand the depths of beauty, I chose to observe women who had a distinct approach to their attractiveness. This observation led to an enlightening realization, where I perceived some women as embodying a kind of floating, in-movement beauty, while others demonstrated a more posed allure. Gleaning insights from these examples contributed significantly to the development of my current theory.

Unleashing the Pinnacle of Your Allure: I am confident that the theory I've created will help you achieve the peak of your unique beauty. It begins with identifying - are you a "Mannequin Beauty" or a "Floating Beauty?" Once you identify yourself, I will present you with a map, a guide to enabling you to attain your utmost beauty potential by tailoring your routine to align with whichever of the two types of beauty you resonate with.

Mannequin Beauty

If you were to draw a line down the center of your face, both halves would be near-perfect reflections of each other, a symmetrical face. Often when you take a selfie picture, you see yourself almost like in the mirror, the picture is what you expected. This type of beauty derives its allure from symmetry, much like the poised elegance of a mannequin. If you study it you consistently find the perfection that lies in symmetry.

How to accent this beauty type:

1. **Center Stage:** Consider parting your hair in the middle. This enhances facial symmetry and provides a visual guideline for others to appreciate your immense perfection on both sides.

2. **Straight Hair Triumph:** Love having your hair straight? Yes, you can pull it off like no one other. This style has a unique way of placing a glamorous spotlight on your symmetrical facial features, enhancing their beauty in an oh-so-subtle yet captivating manner.

3. **Precision Masterstroke:** Complement your eyes with a sharp cat-eye liner, further accentuating the balanced harmony of your face. You are the queen of straight lines.

4. **Killer Gaze:** As for photography, a direct gaze into the camera might just be your signature move, a testament to your poised beauty and allure.

Accented	Not Accented

Note: As a "Mannequin Beauty," you have a slight advantage in highlighting what makes you look good. You can use the tips mentioned earlier to accentuate your symmetry and showcase it. However, it's also perfectly fine to embrace the characteristics that make you a "Floating Beauty."

Floating Beauty

If one were to draw a straight line down the center of your face, it would reveal that both sides are not identical, each presenting its unique allure. Perhaps one of your eyes is slightly larger, or your nose leans a little to one side, or there's a slight difference in the volume of your cheeks. These unique features contribute to the harmonious blend of two distinct beauties that form your single countenance. Often, you may find yourself looking more appealing in videos or motion, and when you take selfie pictures, you might think - I don't look like this in real life. This is because two distinct forms of beauty are coexisting within you, each vying for attention. You are not one, there are two of you! This beauty thrives on motion and fluidity, reflection dance. The more you embrace this vivacity and shun looking flat, the more you'll experience a deep-seated sense of charm and confidence within your skin.

How to accent this beauty type:

1. **Alluring Side Part:** Consider shifting your hair part slightly to one side — whichever side best accentuates your features. Aim to embody the un-measurable allure of a moving work of art. Without rigid lines to be gauged by, your beauty remains a captivating enigma.

2. **Dynamic Hair:** Opt for waves in your hair to introduce a sense of fluidity to your look, enhancing your beauty through the illusion of constant motion. You will come across as an enchanting, floating goddess.

3. **Softened Gaze:** When applying your eye makeup, favor smudged lines. Even if it's a cat-eye look, soften it up. Don't leave the lines sharp, instead create a natural, smoky effect.

4. **Eyebrow Naturalism:** Regarding your eyebrows, allowing them to maintain a more natural shape, free from sharp lines, might enhance your overall look. Perhaps a more naturally styled eyebrow is what highlights your beauty the most, avoiding the overly sculpted "Pomade Brows."

5. **Glowing Goddess:** Infuse your complexion with radiance. Add shine drops to your foundation and combine your concealer with a highlighting liquid. Let light play with your face, catching and reflecting off every angle, showcasing the vitality of your beauty.

6. **Striking the Pose:** As for photography, introduce a slight twist of your head, and choose which side of your beauty

the camera will capture that day. Remember, the two halves of your face offer unique facets of your beauty—don't let them compete with a direct stare into the camera, instead, showcase them separately.

Accented

Not Accented

Word to Wise: This is not a black-and-white theory. It's crucial to consider the unique attributes of your face, as they introduce an element of unpredictability that can't be calculated. As much as something can work for the vast majority, there are always exceptions. For example, if you are the "Floating Beauty" but have pronounced tear trough lines, using luminous liquids there, can make you look worse.

The "Big Guns" Technique

When the powerful arms embellish your stage, life is as easy as turning a page.

Big Guns...What is That? Your "Big Guns" are the areas of your body that occupy the most space and elements that catch the eye instantly. Our largest organ is the skin, which undoubtedly falls into this category. Simultaneously, our hair also commands significant space, playing an undeniable role in shaping our overall appeal. And in third place, our teeth are undoubtedly part of this influential trio, as a significant player.

Memory Lane:

Pivot: A pivotal moment in my beauty journey happened about four years ago. I had just moved to Ibiza. Days were filled with beach escapes and candlelit dinners with my boyfriend. Beach waves in my newly grown super-long hair, sea salt on my skin, and the island's natural glow transformed my daily routine. The Baltic girl in me had always found solace in the transformative power of a full makeup look. However, the Ibiza sun began to rewrite this narrative.

Date Night Ready: After a long day on the beach, the sun kissed my skin just right, giving me a radiant tan that made my teeth look extra crisp white. We never really ate at home, so I started to get ready for our dinner date. The first step was to apply a shimmery after sun cream and then I continued by styling my hair in luscious locks. For the first time, I was like,

Ha, I don't feel like going heavy on my makeup. That evening, I ditched my usual eyeliner and lipstick routine for just a touch of concealer, mascara, and lip balm.

Aha Moment: At the dinner, my boyfriend showered me with compliments. It was an epiphany moment for me: when your skin and hair are in prime condition, they are contributing to at least 50% of your overall appeal. So my hair, luminous and long, combined with my glowing skin and white teeth smile, stole the show. My "Big Guns" were doing all the heavy lifting that evening.

All You Need: This insight led me to a broader realization. People might not notice minute flaws, like a slightly crooked nose or lips that aren't even on both sides. But they will notice thin, damaged hair, lackluster skin, and stained teeth. Investing time and effort into nurturing your hair and skin can dramatically enhance your appearance, often more so than surgical interventions. Even a Barbie would not be looking like a Barbie if it weren't for healthy hair, nice teeth, and sought-after skin. Believe me when I say that your skin and the lusciousness of your hair could be the real game-changers in your beauty arsenal. No lip liner will make your smile more beautiful than perfect pearl teeth. So, always start with taking care of your "Big Guns." Maybe that's all that you need.

The "Cleopatra Effect"

#creating-new-image

Where it All Started: Cleopatra— the original seductive goddess. She is a perfect inspiration when it comes to the art of how we present ourselves. Have you ever imagined making heads turn like she did? This iconic Egyptian queen didn't just use her beauty to captivate. She fully crafted herself by being strategic. She used her brains, wit, and killer charm, to wrap two major Roman bad boys, Julius Caesar, and Mark Antony, around her little finger. ff

What's the Main Trick?: Cleo transformed herself into a mirage of a woman, something so beautiful and carefully crafted like that time turning herself into Aphrodite, a perfectly crafted vison to seduce. Her charm wasn't all about classic beauty there was much more to it. Stories she spun, the power she held, and those grand entrances left everyone's jaws on the floor! Floating through her Egyptian palace with pure grace.

Takeaway: It is the magic power of transforming yourself using looks. That's why she is an inspiration. It's all about crafting a new shell, a vision to leave others amazed. Based on Cleo's talent to do so, I have named this knowledge the "Cleopatra Effect."

New Energy Source: Feel the buzz that sparks the interest of others. I'm sure you know this feeling - maybe you've experienced it on a small scale. An example: My first kick was when I got highlights in my hair for the first time. And I felt a kind of feminine power enter in me. I couldn't walk past a mirror without admiring my new transformation, and people noticed my high energy and new look, which led to them complimenting me.

Refresh & Radiate: New looks inject freshness, and, Gorgeous, you will glow differently! People are suckers for high-energy vibes, and with a makeover, you're basically the human equivalent of an irresistible magnet. It will be a fresh opportunity for you to reintroduce yourself in the light you choose. Your high-energy frequency will be vibrating off the scale! And if people ask you how you got this glow? Well, refer them to this book, of course!

Crafting Your Dream Persona: Let me tell you, the "Cleopatra Effect" isn't just about slapping on a new shade of lipstick or experimenting with a funky hair color—it's so much more than that. We're talking about a deep-sea dive into the essence of who you are, or rather, who you've always dreamed of being, maybe even just for a season. Picture it as bringing to life a persona so enchanting it could be the main character in a movie. I've journeyed down this transformative path, and let me tell you, the metamorphosis is nothing short of spellbinding.

Mood Board Magic: Imagine sitting in front of your computer, opening a Pinterest tab and blank canvas tab. scrolling through endless images that resonate with your dream persona. A head-to-toe look, to the last detail like the smell of the woman you will embody. Your excitement is palpable; you can almost feel the pixels merging with your soul, shaping you into this incredible new version of yourself. Oh yes, it's as magical as it sounds! I always created avatars of myself on my computer, getting incredibly excited about the new persona I was creating. You have the power to change your style and maybe even your life!

The Lux Dark Femme: For example, you choose to be a lux version of a dark femme. You start by looking at women under these keywords on Pinterest, checking what they are wearing, and screenshot details that fit the most your ideal fantasy and then dragging the images to the blank canvas. Then you choose a dark faux fur coat, mysterious bangs, and a silk slip dress under, with perfect smokey eye makeup. **Fun fact:** fur coats and hair with bangs, this combination is a chef's kiss*.

Insta Queen's Knows: Ready for some scalding-hot tea, Love? If you've been wondering how one of Instagram's most-followed diva slays the game, let's spill: she's been channeling the Cleopatra effect since her teen years, and oh my, **You Know…She Knows!** No, we're not just talking about the curated ensembles or the striking selfies; it's her whole aura—each persona more mesmerizing than the last. In her world, boredom is the only sin. When she drops a new product, she doesn't just "Launch"—she unveils an experience. It's not merely about lip gloss; it's a new mood, a vibe, an entire epic story in a tube! And she morphs herself into this product launch-carrying goddess with a whole new look.

Time to Unleash the "Cleopatra Effect:" When you're feeling drained or disconnected from the vibrant thrum of life, it's time to channel Cleopatra. Perhaps you're standing at the brink of a new chapter or yearning to add a pinch of exotic spice to your relationship, allowing your partner to discover you in a completely different light. You might not have the bandwidth to deploy the "Cleopatra Effect" as frequently as our "Insta Queen," nor may you need to, but let there be no doubt—whenever you feel the pull to disrupt your universe and tap into a new energy grid, it's your cue to unleash your inner Cleopatra moment.

Recipe

1. **Inspiration Hunt:** Kick off your Cleo journey by launching a blank canvas on your computer. Flick open another tab and dive into an aesthetic picture website like Pinterest.

2. **Who Will You Be?:** Submerge yourself in an ocean of images and let them inspire you. Who do you aspire to be? Maybe it's by Cleopatra herself in a modern-day setting, or even better use this book as your inspiration starting point.

3. **Character Craft:** Start curating your chosen dream woman's archetype. Copy and paste pictures of outfits, haircuts, accessories, makeup looks, and perfumes until you create a full ensemble.

4. **Fantasy Traits:** Perhaps even write down traits you aspire to acquire or enhance within yourself that go hand in hand with your new avatar. For example, being bold or unapologetic, it's a good way to start your power journey.

5. **Bring it to Life:** One of the last stages in this transformational journey involves fully embracing the persona you've created. It may entail reorganizing your wardrobe, selling off old clothing to finance new pieces, scheduling a hair makeover, and mastering the art of makeup that will showcase your new persona.

6. **Be the Woman:** Walk, talk, and look like the persona you've designed. After all, you are what you create!

The "Celebrity Doppelgänger" Trick

#Copying-celibrity-style-clone

Star Power: Are you prepared to strut down the metaphorical red carpet? Visualize yourself receiving fashion guidance from the crème de la crème of the style industry. Welcome to the exciting realm of the "Celebrity Doppelgänger" technique. You might wonder, what is Doppelgänger? It's a memorable way to say a person that looks just like you, aka a copy of you. Admittedly, it might not be everyone's cup of tea, but for many, it's a veritable treasure trove of inspiration and undeniably worth exploring. Have you ever been compared to a celebrity? If so, who? This task might not be a breeze for everyone; not all of us can pinpoint our Hollywood lookalikes with ease. However, my Dear, I'm confident that there's a star out there whose looks resonate with your reflection - I can certainly identify a few for myself!

Memory Lane:

Hot Beverage Chat: The memory transports me back to a cozy encounter last year. Picture this: me and my bestie, nestled in our favorite café, our chatter punctuated by the comforting hum of our steaming drinks. Out of the blue, she tells me I have high fashion doppelgängers and how I seem like a perfect blend of these two famous models. I smiled and didn't think much of it at the moment.

Let's Explore: However, that night, as I cozied up in my bed, the thought started to tickle my curiosity. "Could we really be that similar?" I found myself delving into the world of Pinterest to investigate. As I scrolled through their snapshots, I was captivated, it was like peering into a stylish mirror! "Wow, that outfit screams me!" and "Oh, that unique blend of styles— simply irresistible!" The thought of replicating their looks, attempting their makeup artistry, and sporting their hairstyles started to brew in my mind. And since then it has become my go-to style therapy, a delightful pastime of gathering fashion inspiration.

Digital Treasure Chest: Even now, I carefully curate a folder, continually adding and subtracting from my favorite images. So, whenever there's an event looming, or when I crave a dose of inspiration, I dive into this digital treasure chest I've created. I owe a flirtatious wink to their stylists, thank you for your magical touch. Trust me, it's doing wonders for my style!

Stealing the Best: With that all being said, I invite you to steal elements of style from your doppelgänger that resonate the most with you. It's like they paid a stylist, and this stylist gave both of you solutions to elevate your look. This approach may not revolve around complete imitation, but rather, it's about siphoning off those sparkling elements that deeply resonate with your personal style.

Just Like Designing your Home: Think of this strategy as borrowing inspiration for your personal space. Often, people scour similar spaces already designed, picking elements that resonate with their vision.

Recipe

1. **Your Celeb Match:** Find your celebrity. There are even apps for it. Ensure you share similarities in complexion, body type, facial features, or even hair and eye color. A 55% match minimum.

2. **The Right Era:** Aim for the phase when your chosen celebrity was in their "Slay" era. Avoid their "Flop" eras!

3. **Heartbeat Moments:** Go through images or videos of the celebrity until you find looks that make your heart race. Focus on their appearances at interviews, casual events, or even sports events. Bypass extreme versions of red carpet looks or paparazzi shots from their "Sloppy" days.

4. **Detail Dive:** Once you've collated a set of inspirational images, it's time to dive deep. Go ahead, and examine their hairstyles, makeup choices, colors they often wear, and even accessories. Whole combination.

5. **Adapt and Apply:** With your notes in hand, begin to experiment. Embrace their looks into your style. The magic is in the fusion of their style and your personality.

Word to Wise: Stay away from extremes, such as sporting a half-shaved head or donning bright blue hair, unless they truly reflect who you are.

"*Je Ne Sais Quoi*"
Effects

In the following pages, you will find easy-to-follow combinations; if you choose one, you will leave an extremely seductive impression. For each one of these looks, I have tried out their effectiveness firsthand.

The "White Button-Down Effect"

Refined and Sexy

Fasten your Seatbelt, Gorgeous, we're About to Take Off:
We're diving straight into this chapter with one of the sexiest examples I can provide. This iconic look has served me well over the years, and I'm confident it will continue to be a timeless "Ace Card" for many more.

Memory Lane:

Star in the Crowd: Okay, picture this: I'm at a club, surrounded by a sea of classic party dresses, spending time with beautiful souls, living my best life. Then enters my new friend, as usually late- rocking a crisp white button-down paired with a chic black A-line skirt, hair in Hollywood locks swept to one side, killer black pumps, and red lips paired with otherwise neutral makeup. And believe me, it was as if she'd tapped into some hidden reservoir of magnetism. The moment she stepped into the room, all eyes were irresistibly drawn to her—It was as though she was a magnetic seductress, pulling everyone into her aura, unable to look away.

Sophisticated Meets Sexy: On that particular evening I understood that the button-down wasn't just a shirt; it was a little sprinkle of "*Je Ne Sais Quoi.*" There she was, sipping her dirty martini, looking confident and put-together amidst the short dresses, sequins, and glitter. It screamed, "I know what I'm doing, and I look sexy while doing it." This is not your regular party attire, but wow, did it make an impression? The attire unmistakably projected the dazzling undertone of professional and intellectual hotness, which gave her superiority over the club's atmosphere.

What Makes it HOT: I have understood, by using this effective combo repeatedly. The charm lies in the interplay of the serious versus the flirty. The white button-down shirt is typically associated with business meetings and formal settings- serious occasions requiring sophistication. When you take it into a playful atmosphere, it becomes a character you play, by creating a narrative in people's brains. The star of the narrative is the compelling interplay between serious sophistication and playful sensuality. Its unique ability to foster an air of desire while preserving its refined elegance sets it apart in the world of seductive garments. The crisp collar, the fitted silhouette, the hint of skin visible between buttons— these elements work together to create an aesthetic that's both respectful and risqué.

Occasion: Fashion Alchemy, Gorgeous! This look is your sartorial wand, easily transforming you from that office boss to a woman exemplifying sophisticated seductiveness while having a glass of dirty martini. It can even turn you into a sultry siren for a steamy date night. No need for an outfit change—just stamp on a bold red lip. Fashionable yet practical? Now, that's a combo every modern enchantress can get behind.

Recipe

1. **Staple:** Slip into your flawlessly tailored, crisp white button-down- the fit is just right, neither too loose nor oversized. Forget about any embellished variants; we maintain a seriously classy aesthetic here.

2. **Skirt or Spice:** Your perfect go-to mix is with a black A-line skirt, but if you're feeling a little bit naughty, consider a black leather mini-skirt. But if you feel devilish on a particular day, then the black leather pants will fit your vibe the best.

3. **Heel Yeah!:** Step into your go-to black pumps, classic and chic. Opt for classic leather or patent leather. Your second option would be black and clean-looking high-heeled strappy sandals.

4. **Lip Action:** Swipe that ravishing red lipstick to bring out your inner Siren. It will make your lips pop, juxtaposing against the white button-down. Pucker up, Gorgeous!

5. **Bling, but Make it Subtle:** If you're craving a necklace, go with something dainty—no heavy-duty stuff here. We are keeping things "Professional."

6. **Hair Flair:** Unleash those locks or whip up a flirty curled ponytail. Keep the hairstyle classy and polished! Note: Never let your hair tie to be seen.

7. **Wrists:** Strap on an elegant watch. Forget stacked-up bracelets; you're a woman with time and style on her side. One single accessory on the wrist is all you need.

8. **Nails:** No questions here, red or nude shades only.

The "Long Sport-Socks Effect"

Playful Seduction

In your long hosiery, you're a queen, the finest one they've ever seen.

How to Make Others Sweat?: Ever pondered how to make other people in the gym break a sweat, just by looking at you? Fear not, Gorgeous, I've got your back with the sassiest attire tip. Make your next gym visit a showstopper, turning heads and garnering that extra prolonged glance your way.

Memory Lane:

Meet Her: A few years back, my best friend embarked on a new journey as a fitness guru. Naturally, I was intrigued to see her in her new environment and decided to visit her at the gym one day. Dressed in what I believed to be a rather alluring ensemble of form-fitting leggings and a flattering sports bra, I felt hot. However, upon my arrival, I was taken aback by besties' attire. She greeted me at the door donned in a cropped loose white top, skintight biker shorts, and her pièce de résistance[2]- long sports socks.

Prolonged Stares: As she guided me through the maze of gym equipment, I couldn't help but notice that all eyes were on her. I wondered what was so captivating about her... before it dawned on me - it was her long socks. They enhanced her athletic charm, making her look incredibly sexy. I think we all have heard about "Long Socks Fetish," it might be more popular than you think. I candidly commended her unique fashion sense that day, pointing out that she might be onto

---

[2] pièce de résistance: Most important or exciting thing

37

something with those socks. Since then, she has made it her signature style, being the hosiery siren of the wellness world.

I'm Taking It Home: I realized this is something to take home with you. Whenever I want to look extremely sexy, I add a pair of long socks to my gym wear combo.

Occasion: Anytime, Darling, when you desire an extra admiring look at the gym. Maybe there is someone special in the gym that you are trying to get noticed by.

Recipe

1. **Choose the Base:** Opt for mini loose sports shorts or mini biker shorts.

2. **Top it Up:** Choose a sports bra, loose cropped top, or body-fitting long-sleeved one.

3. **Hair Down?:** If you want to have your beautiful hair down, just pop on a sweat headband, for that extra hair whip.

4. **Here Comes the "Bad Boys":** Get those long sexy, almost knee-high socks on.

5. **Color Theory:** Remember Gorgeous, it's fundamental to coordinate your sock color with either your top or bottom. Avoid introducing a third color into your outfit, as it can disrupt the overall harmony. Staying within the same color palette is crucial to looking alluring.

The "Tiffany's Effect"

Sophisticated Allure

The Tiffany Epiphany: This one is for you elegance-loving Goddess! I've got to spill the tea on something that's been a game-changer for me—the undeniable magic I call the "Tiffany's Effect."

Memory Lane:

The "Breakfast at Tiffany's" Awakening: During the research phase for my design school project, I immersed myself in the vintage cinema world, exploring fashion history. It wasn't long before I stumbled upon what arguably stands as the most iconic of all... Breakfast at Tiffany's. While analyzing the main character suddenly, I realized -**"You Know...She Knows."**

Killer Trio: I understood it was never about the opulent jewelry or the couture gowns. It was the unerring integrity of character that Hepburn brought to her roles, and quite simply replicating formula: The iconic black dress, the jet-black sunglasses, the pearls—it was the magic potion.

You Don't Need a Million to Look Like a Million: Here's the secret, my stunning woman: you don't need a top designer to channel your inner Audrey. A simple black dress, a pair of killer heels, pearl earrings/necklace, the quintessential jet-black sunglasses, and the finishing touch? An updo that Audrey herself would applaud. That's all it takes. Each piece is individually affordable. Together? Priceless. That's "Je Ne Sais

Quoi" for you—the allure that's indefinable but undeniably present. It's an epiphany that has transformed not just my wardrobe but also the way I perceive fashion and elegance. There's something incredibly empowering about that, isn't it?

Alchemy of the Ensemble: It's all in the details, Gorgeous. The beauty of this look is the way each element plays its part. The sunglasses add that dash of mystery elegance to you, while the dark top acts as a sophisticated backdrop, so you can shine—and the pearls? Oh, they're the cherries on top. They add that irreplaceable touch of luxury flirt that makes the whole ensemble sing. If you're not a fan of pearls, you can opt for a gold accessory set that will shine beautifully around your ears or neck. Just a friendly reminder: use classic-style gold accessories, and stay away from multiple layers of chains, as they will clash with the overall look.

The Compliment Cascade: Prepare to be the focal point. You'll find that the compliments will pour in like champagne at a soiree, people raving about your sophisticated charm.

Occasion: City Lights and Starry Nights! Gorgeous, this look is your go-to when you're aiming to channel that "Main Character" aura for formal events or city escapades. It screams sophistication and a well-curated life. Remember: this look is more of a "Champagne in the Afternoon" than a "Popcorn and Soda " kinda look.

Recipe

1. **Black Top that Speaks Volumes:** Whether it's a cozy turtleneck or a classic **LBD**,[3] make sure it's in a luxurious dark hue and has a classic elegance to it.

2. **Neckline:** The boat neckline is top-tier for this look. However, if you have another top that screams elegance, it's completely fine.

3. **Pearl It Up:** Go for a pair of pearl earrings, a delicate pearl necklace, or even both.

4. **Don't do Pearls?:** No worries Gorgeous, consider choosing classy, round-shaped stud earrings that are made of gold. Or a luxury-looking gold necklace.

5. **The Sunglasses Factor:** Don your chicest pair of jet-black sunglasses. Make sure they're in a classic shape to ooze that timeless allure. Your shades aren't just about shielding those pretty eyes from the sun; they're about adding an air of put-together elegance.

6. **Hair Majesty:** Tuck those locks into an elegant updo—chignon, twist, or bun, you choose! The goal here is to ensure your hairstyle exudes a touch of refinement. If a ponytail is your chosen style, ensure that you disguise the elastic by artfully wrapping a strand of your hair around it and securing the end with a chic French pin.

7. **Walk the Walk:** Step out with the poise and grace of a Hollywood legend, you are an icon now.

---

3 LBD- stands for little black dress.

The "Eternal Bride" Aura

Symbolic Hypnosis

Under the sparkling mantle of white, may your dreams sway in a delicate waltz.

Memory Lane:

Two Girls and a Very Big City: Let's time travel back: I'm in my early twenties, moving to a bustling metropolis like Shanghai with my newfound instant best friend. We're two models who only worked in Europe before coming to Asia, but we enjoyed navigating our way through a carefree and fun lifestyle in a completely new environment. Since we were sharing a cozy room together it also meant sharing one wardrobe. Our nights were filled with adventures, and we reveled in styling each other for each evening's escapades.

Running Gag: One day, I purchased a white jumpsuit so elegant, that it was akin to a wedding gown. The same day before heading for our classic night out I showed it to my friend. She had a spark of inspiration, suggesting, "Let's style you as a bride tonight." She adorned me with long, dazzling Swarovski crystal earrings and a delicate tennis necklace, then she added, "All you need now is an elegant updo and white strappy heels." So, I agreed to play the bride for the night. The outfit was sublime, and once we arrived at the trendiest bar in Shanghai, I felt like a celebrity, who was looked at from every corner. As you might expect, the drinks were on me that evening. The "Bride" look was a hit, sparking curious admiration and compliments. It dawned on me - this could be a thing. Next was my friend's turn to don the bridal ensemble, and her experience mirrored mine. From then on, the running gag was guessing who would be the next bride for the next night out and secure us free drinks all night.

Eternal Choice: Sometimes, the greatest life hacks and style tips don't come from flashy magazines or celeb Instagram accounts but from what's right in front of us. One of the most iconic events and outfits is a bride's gown. In this world of fast fashion and fleeting trends, the white dress proves that some style lessons are, indeed, eternal.

Personal Preference: Since not everyone finds the traditional concept of marriage in a white gown appealing, it's important to acknowledge that the ceremony itself can carry historical implications, and if that is triggering to you, feel free to skip this chapter, Gorgeous.

Collective Mind: The look of a bride has left an indelible imprint on our collective consciousness. You can use this influential symbolism to your benefit, crafting a captivating narrative with the "Bride Effect" to create attraction with a snap of your fingers. And you know the looks you will get that night will be like people subconsciously are seeing the bride.

White Color: The most iconic color that represents a bride. It's the color of heaven, or at least it can make you heavenly.

Crystal Waterfall: To complement this ethereal ensemble, think—a crystal or diamond accessory that serves as a whispering accompaniment. Perhaps it's a pair of diamond studs or teardrop crystals that catch the light just so right.

Occasion: This look is your VIP ticket to those black-tie soirees, opulent city dinners, and ritzy holiday get-togethers. Or if you plan to go to a lounge bar or a club, skip the dress and be ready to be the center of attention, wearing a heavenly jumpsuit.

Recipe

1. **The Dress:** Seek a white dress or jumpsuit that favors elegance over extravagance.

2. **Length:** Keep it long and classic, putting the wow effect on a long slit in a dress or a neckline that shows off your collar bones.

3. **Clean:** Keep it fitted and clean-looking, with no embellishments. That will leave the space for your body's allure points to carry sparkling embellishments.

4. **Choose Your Sparkle:** Opt for the shiniest bling you can get, like Swarovski crystals, or if it's in your budget go for diamonds.

5. **Bridal Hair:** Embrace a timeless elegance with this hairstyle. A simple yet sophisticated look is the key to nailing this bridal style. Whether it's a curled ponytail or a neat chignon, the more elegant, the better.

6. **Harmonize:** Think about how each element interacts. Every piece should feel like a note in a harmonious melody.

Unlocking the "Skin-On-Skin" Illusion

Paint a dance in their vision's heart. Keep this secret your silent art.

Showstopper: Let's talk about a seductive look that stops people in their tracks—the secret potion called the "Skin-on-Skin" Technique. An ensemble so aligned with your natural skin tone that it becomes an extension of you, turning every street into a runway and you, Gorgeous, into the showstopper. This is not just about looking good; this is artistry, this is "*Je Ne Sais Quoi*" in sartorial form.

Memory Lane:

Very Sexy Learning Experience: Just another day in fashion design school, expecting just another day of patterns, fabric, sketches, and silhouettes. I never predicted that the day's lessons would shake me to my very core as a "Femme Fatale Detective." As I was setting my table up for work, I turned around and saw my classmate sauntering into the classroom in a silky, light brown dress that seemed as if it were spun from her very essence. The dress flaunted her legs and laid effortlessly on her like a second skin. It was almost as if the fabric was an extension of her, but just one shade lighter than her natural skin tone.

Her Glow Secret: The first thing I said was, wow, your skin, is so glowy. She unveiled the mystery that lay beneath her luminous skin: a daily anointment with shea butter that lent it a soft, celestial glow. As the fabric of her attire pirouetted with her skin tone in a captivating ballet, it was impossible to look away.

What Makes "Skin-on-Skin" So Special: The secret to this technique is harmony. It's about creating an outfit that looks as if your skin is swathed in another layer of itself but slightly darker/lighter, so it would create a slight contrast. Imagine a dress or blouse so perfectly matched in hue and undertone to your skin that the two harmonize, each making the other more vibrant and alive. The technique creates a balance, a unity between garment and skin, which is arresting.

Trials and Triumphs: When I first attempted to replicate this sorcery, I found it a bit challenging to find that perfect shade, that ideal fabric that could capture the same undertone as my skin. Once I found it, it became one of my favorite summer date night looks with my partner. And Uff, the way he adored the "Skin-on-Skin" effect on me.

This Is Your Spotlight: Why go for the ordinary when you can have the extraordinary? The "Skin-On-Skin" technique is more than a fashion statement; it's a dialogue between you and the world, announcing your sex appeal in a brilliantly curated manner.

Occasion: Dial up the charm; this look is custom-made for any setting where a little flirting is not only allowed but encouraged! Be it a first date or the tenth date, this ensemble sets the stage for love—or at least a delightful conversation. Unveil your playful side and make every occasion a chance for romance.

Recipe

1. **Nude Dress:** Choose a nude dress that's one shade darker/lighter than your skin tone for a subtle yet sultry "Second skin" effect. A silky or satin finish will add an irresistible allure to the overall look. The dress should be designed to display your arms, legs, and possibly décolletage for a captivating touch of tasteful charm.

2. **Unveiling the Canvas:** The beauty of "Skin-on-Skin" elegance lies in the dewy glow of well-moisturized skin. Prep yourself the day before by indulging in a lavish shea butter treatment before bed. On the day, repeat the shea butter application to maintain a soft, hydrated look. Just remember, consistency is the secret to this luxurious routine.

3. **All About the Shoes:** To complete the look, opt for nude shoes that match the dress. This will subtly elongate your figure, creating a sophisticated silhouette that's undeniably chic.

4. **Elevate your Bedroom Charm:** This technique also holds immense potential for creating a sultrily appealing look for intimate moments. If a romantic evening with your significant other is on the agenda, try implementing this strategy in your lingerie drawer.

Word to Wise: However, let it be noted that this effect is made for deeper skin tones; it brings out a richness and depth that is simply captivating. So if you have medium-tan to deep complexions, it will work magic.

The "White Tee Revelation"

Casually Sexy

In a simple white shirt, your radiant gleam, a treasured memory like a dream.

The Casual Bombshell Phenomenon: Listen closely, Gorgeous, because what I'm about to share is the women's answer to that hilarious male phenomenon known as the "Gray Sweatpants" allure. And let's face it, we've all heard about how those unassuming gray sweatpants have a strange, almost mythical, chokehold on our eyes. Well, Sister, we have our own power-play, and it's JUST as effortless, casual, and simple as putting gray sweatpants on.

Memory Lane:

The Accidental Awakening: Picture it—my late teens, still navigating the labyrinth of style and appeal. While I was visiting my best friend in London, I had my first step into a world-famous lingerie store. There I picked up a perfect round push-up bra. It was not intentional, okay, a little bit, but who doesn't want her breasts to look bigger being a teenage girl? Once I returned to my school, I paired it with a crisp white T-shirt that hugged me so tight! And then, an "A-ha" moment in style appeal unfolds. All the looks and compliments I got from boys/girls in the school were crazy. To this day, I appreciate this combination coz no matter how many years pass by, it always works! Simple, casual, but oh-so transformative!

The "White Tee Effect" Decoded: Ladies, trust me when I say that the blend of a smooth, rounded bra underneath a snug white tee is a coded siren's call. The magic lies in the effortlessness of it—the "I was not even trying" vibe that, paradoxically, makes you irresistibly radiant. And the fabric of the T-shirt? Impeccably soft and hugging your curves. The result? Your breasts appear as two perfect half-moons, making you a low-key knockout.

Girl Next Door: This ensemble has such a "Girl Next Door" sex appeal aura to it. It's if you're not even trying, yet still capturing attention. The snug, white tee delivers a crisp, fresh aesthetic, while the perfectly rounded bra does all the nuanced work.

Universal Validation: If you're doubting the ubiquity of this phenomenon, let me just say that the TikTok community confirmed my theory in droves! I dropped a video discussing this very topic, and voila, a torrent of women chimed in, nodding in virtual agreement on how many compliments this simple look has gotten them. Seems like this casual bombshell look has international appeal.

Occasion: Girl next door charm unleashed! Ideal for those laid-back dates, school, trips to the cinema, or visiting a basketball game where your man/woman is playing. This look is your go-to. Essentially, it's your style's secret weapon for those moments when you want to look fabulous but make it look easy.

Recipe

1. **The Right Bra:** Opt for one that promotes a seamless, impeccably rounded silhouette. Avoid bras with teardrop shapes, reliefs, or so-called t-shirt bras. What you need is a full-cup bra that provides a supremely rounded shape— ensure it resembles more of a perfect circle rather than an egg shape. As well you can opt for padding for an optimal boost.

2. **White Tee Magic:** Look out for a form-fitting crisp white tee made of sumptuously soft fabric that hugs you and your two God-given "Blessings."

3. **White Color:** It's important to understand what kind of white color complements you the most. Is it warm white, or cold white?

4. **Optional Add-Ons:** If you don't feel comfy in a tight fit in other places, layer it with a casual cardigan or an unbuttoned flannel shirt to keep the focus where it counts.

5. **Assemble it:** wear it with blue color jeans, skirts, and shorts. Even black leggings pair with it nicely, keeping it casual and sporty.

6. **Rock Your Confidence:** The look isn't complete without your killer smile. Own it, Gorgeous!

Word to Wise: This fashion hack might not be everyone's cup of tea. If form-fitting clothes make you uneasy, that's perfectly okay. Always honor your individual style sensibility because being comfortable in your own skin epitomizes allure at its finest!

The "Angelic Effect"

Ethereally Captivating

Ready to glow like an ethereal goddess? Just say: "Yes, I'm heavenly fabulous."

Oh, Divine Goddess: Imagine walking into a room and everyone's like, "Who's that Celestial Goddess?" Yes, that's the vibe for the "Angelic Look." This ensemble is all about ethereal elegance, infusing your aura with a soft, heavenly glow. With this **"Angelic Look,"** you're not just present in the room; you elevate the energy of the room.

Memory Lane:

So, let's Rewind to This: A breezy seaside concert and the mood is straight-up enchanting. There I am, sixteen and just dipping my toes into the glam world of femininity. I mean, really, when I think back, I was so young! As I strutted toward the bar area, BOOM! Time froze. **"You Know...She Knows"** Sipping her white wine by the bar, this ethereal beauty had us all in a trance. Picture a long, one-shouldered vanilla white dress, skin that whispered of summer's golden hues, and cascading honey-colored locks that kissed her waist. And, oh, that makeup? Subtle yet spellbinding—think mascara-touched eyes with twinkling inner corners and a lip color that gleamed every time she sipped her chilled white wine with such elegance. She was an absolute vision! Truly radiating beauty.

Caught in the Gaze: Our poor waiter? He tried to play it cool, but those glazed eyes gave him away. Even with her handsome hubby by her side, everyone's gaze was unapologetically glued to her. And honestly? Same. She was the epitome of celestial charm. By looking at her, you could tell, she had an intentional look. I hope her husband was not the jealous type. If that's the case, he would have lived a tough life, considering how alluring **She knew** to make herself look. And that's how the "Angelic Woman" was imprinted in my mind—radiant, celestial, timeless, and mesmerizing.

Full Circle: Fast forward a year, and I'm prepping for this big event. You bet I had that "Angel" as my inspiration. Dark curls, flowing off-white dress, and that perfectly placed self-tanner. And, of course, I opted for a highlighter to accentuate all the right places – shoulders, eyes, cheekbones, and that kissable cupid's bow. I had lash extensions, which perfectly complemented the natural and subtle lash look. Oh, and those nude heels with ankle ties? Felt like I was prancing on clouds. (BTW, black shoes are a total crime for this vibe. They kind of drag the look down. Go for anything extra light and feminine.)

A Night to Remember!: And wow, did the evening deliver! It went perfectly. I felt feminine and attractive; maybe I subconsciously embodied the woman I saw last year. And I won't lie, the praises were pouring in. When a random girl stops by to gush over your look, that's the universe giving you a gold star. Trust me, one compliment from a woman is equal to three compliments from a man.

Staple for Life: I still rock that look—whenever I'm in the mood for some admiration. A little sprinkle of self-love, you know? And it's not about being vain or anything. I mean, we're all multifaceted gems! Just like I adore making my living space fabulous, I see myself as this ever-evolving canvas. Paint, glitter, shine—I'm here for it all. Celebrating and being celebrated!

Occasion: Garden Soirees and Seaside Serenades ah, envision yourself amidst floral blossoms and ocean breezes. This look is your go-to for those sun-kissed garden parties and whimsical seaside events. So, whether you're sipping on champagne or strolling by the sea, you'll be the embodiment of ethereal charm.

Recipe

1. **Hair Vibes:** Opt for "Angelic Hair." (Hair recipe on page 80).

2. **Dream Dress:** Step into that divine white or off-white ensemble—long, airy, with flirty details like a one-shoulder, off-shoulder, or oh-so-enchanting open-back moment.

3. **Sparkle Central:** Illuminate those shoulders and collarbones with a dash of celestial highlighter.

4. **Sun-Kissed:** Skip the contour today, honey. We're aiming for that soft, angelic glow. Maybe just a dust of golden shimmer bronzer? Absolutely! Just to channel those golden rays.

5. **Cheeky Shine:** Give your cheekbones the spotlight with a quick swipe of that luminous highlighter. The same goes for Cupid's bow make it glimmer with a slight touch.

6. **Eye Magic:** Slip some champagne eyeshadow for those lids and twinkle those inner corners. Cheers, Beauty!

7. **Step on Clouds:** The finishing step is the light-colored heels-think straps and ankle bows. A heavenly match to float on!

Red-Hot Details

- **Goddess Feet:** Never underestimate the allure of well-groomed toes. A French pedicure takes you from everyday clean to otherworldly temptress. Adorn your impeccably groomed feet with an anklet, adding a dash of whimsical allure to your appearance.

- **Scent-Sational Vibes:** Whether you go for the comforting aroma of vanilla or the invigorating scent of "Paradise Garden, [4]" you should opt for leaving a beautiful trail of aura as you move, bound to be memorable.

- **Unhook the Conventions #FreeTheNip:** Skip the bra for an effortless, airy vibe that communicates confidence and comfort in your skin. It's a bold choice that aligns with the unapologetic choice to feel liberated and confident which is beyond sexy.

---

[4] Paradise Garden scent : You can find this mix in page 126

The "Hot Boss"
Juxtaposition

Get set. It's a captivating chokehold so divine and so bold.

A True Style Statement!: If I had to nail what is "Hot Boss" for you in one sentence, it would be a Juxtaposition of feminine against masculine. Now, let's deep dive into this audacious style that's so close to my heart and, hopefully, soon to be yours.

What's the Vibe?: The "Hot Boss" look seamlessly merges commanding allure with an undeniably sultry femineity. Think of it as a harmonious dance between power and sensuality. The allure of this style stems from its fusion of conventional business attire, often seen as daunting, with a feminine twist that results in an unapologetically sexy statement.

Balancing Act: While skin might be on display, the key is to harmonize it with elements that scream respect. Regardless of your choice, the "Hot Boss" aura guarantees a magnetic presence that resonates with assertiveness and the capability to make a "Rise to the Occasion" for anyone. Wink*

Memory Lane:

NYE: Oh, let me take you back to a New Year's Eve that still gives me chills—a defining "Hot Boss" moment that was nothing short of electrifying. Picture this: a room full of sparkling dresses and tailored tuxedos, a sea of conventional glamour. Then, she walked in, my dear friend, and instantly, the room went from lit to on fire!

She Dressed to Impress!: Garbed in a sleek, polished black pantsuit, she made every head turn and every jaw drop. Her black structured blazer was flawlessly complemented by a crisp white blouse that screamed elegance. To accent her feminine figure, she had chosen a belt that screamed dominance. Her hands were adorned with sparkling sleeve gloves that gave her a magical touch. But wait, here comes the twist that had everyone captivated—a man's tie, cinched neatly around her neck, shattering norms and stealing the spotlight. It was as if she was daring the world to define her, playing with the boundaries between traditional masculinity and saturated femininity.

Goldilocks: Her golden tresses weren't just flowing; they were cascading like a waterfall of liquid gold down her shoulders, each strand reflecting the room's ambient glow. Her hair was playing a juxtaposition game, letting them be as glamorously feminine as they could be against the structured blazer's shoulders. Her lips? Painted a tantalizing, deep crimson that added just the right touch of passionate flair. When she moved, people didn't just look; they stared, ensnared by the compelling force that was her "Hot Boss" look. Men were intrigued, women were inspired, and everyone was, well, a bit smitten. It was more than an outfit; it was a look where even traditionally heterosexual women had lady-loving intrigue for a brief, fleeting night.

Electric Charge: You could feel the electric charge in the air, proving that the woman does not always need to show her skin to be seductive. And that, my friends, was when I realized the real power of the "Hot Boss" aesthetic—it has room in a chokehold. The message is clear: **"You Know…She Knows."**

Hot Boss Testing: That night, after witnessing her captivating charm, I was eager to recreate her effortless allure. However, with no upcoming occasions to dress up for, I felt a touch of disappointment. That was until later in the week when a friend reached out for fashion advice. She had a work event to attend and confessed that she was genuinely interested in her company's owner – not for any unscrupulous reason, but simply because she had a genuine crush on him and he was single. After hearing her story and the significance of the event, an idea sparked in my mind. I assured her that I had the perfect fashion strategy for her event.

Let's Style You Baby: I helped her assemble an outfit consisting of a transparent lace bodysuit with a deep V cut beneath a structured, one-button blazer, black suit pants, and striking black pumps. For added allure, I recommended red lipstick and her hair styled in glamorous Hollywood waves. When she sent me pre-event photos, she looked absolutely stunning. As fate would have it, she not only interacted with her company's owner, but he also showed significant interest in her. What turned out to be a massive turn-off for her that night. She is "Just a Girl" and you know how it happens to us girls, once we achieve our desires, they might give us an ick. Nevertheless, that night's success served as a testament to the power of a carefully curated, irresistible "Hot Boss" look.

Occasion: Depending on how spicy you dial up this "Hot Boss" ensemble, it can even sashay into the office—just be sure to keep it on the sophisticated side of sexy. This look is especially perfect for events where you aim to showcase your powerful allure. Whether it's a night to stand out or a business party, consider your vibe set to be unforgettable. Beware that leaning too much into the masculine aspect of the "Hot Boss" aesthetic could be excessively daunting on a first date.

Recipe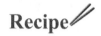

1. **Boss Attire:** Opt for outfits that scream - business meeting, as the foundation of your outfit. Like a black pantsuit with sharp, strong shoulders. Topped with a man-sized watch and a black tie. For Those all-white affairs opt for something like an elegant white blazer dress.

2. **Ultra-Feminine Tease:** Find your extra feminine juxtaposition against the boss's attire in a way that makes you feel the best. It can be a lace body suit under that boss blazer paired with a feminine hairstyle. It can be a structured button vest against bare skin. Even it can be a tight white blouse with a black tie, as long as you have feminine cherry on top of the look.

3. **Tailored Temptation:** The secret to a fiery look is a well-cut outfit. Adapt your formal wear to hug your figure just right, fitting you as seamlessly as a glove. Opt for structured cuts. Loose blouses are not welcome here.

4. **Killer Bag:** Go for sharply defined bags that ooze respect. Opt for a design with a firm silhouette, in colors: Red or Black.

5. **Command the Room with Color:** To truly encapsulate the essence of a commanding seduction ruler, the color palette of your ensemble must be powerful and profound. Consider opulent shades such as pristine white, mysterious black, and deep navy blue. Gray can also be a potent choice, but only if you can pull it off. But don't forget the vibrant streak of bold red, acting as a statement color.

6. **Heels of Ardor:** Pair of killer black pumps. Power dressing is as much about the shoes as it is about the clothes.

Red-Hot Details

- **Bold Femme:** Pair this ensemble with either fiery red lips or nails, amplifying the saturated femme beneath the sculpted blazer.

- **Hair Juxtaposition:** Since the outfit is very masculine, make sure your hair is super feminine, for that magic to take place.

- **Bare the Skin:** Imagine a sharp vest, bearing your skin underneath, or a blazer. This ensemble exudes sex appeal.

- **Escalate the Dynamics:** envisage the incorporation of a robust, masculine wristwatch. The stark juxtaposition of this audacious accessory against your feminine body. It's daring, it's provocative—a clear message about who's the "Hot Boss."

- **Pleasure Fusion:** Perhaps you're already familiar with this tantalizing secret, but if not, prepare for a revelation. The seductive dance between masculine and feminine fragrances becomes an irresistibly appealing forbidden tango, intertwining the robust notes of a masculine perfume with the spicy sweetness of a personal feminine scent. This intoxicating fusion is guaranteed to leave a trail of alluring aftereffects.

- **Confidence Boost:** The confidence that power dressing instills is the ultimate accessory.

The "Hot Library" Tease

Smart Seduction

Amidst the library's hushed scene, she exists, a vision serene, a sultry mirage to be captured, where wisdom and silence are raptured.

What's Behind It?: It's when you're dressed modestly enough for study, but potent enough to kindle a spark of desire. This is your hypnotic charm of "Library Hot". It creates a compelling vision of being immersed in the tranquil environment of a library, subtly emitting an irresistible aura of seductress that you can truly be.

Envision This...

Peek-a-Boo: As **"You Know...She Knows"** steps into the library, she is a sight to behold, adorned in a finely knitted ensemble, ohh but wait, has she left her bra at home? The over-knee fitted skirt, coupled with a sweater jacket, is an elegant selection. The daring allure of her outfit is heightened by the dual-button fixture at the top of her jacket. Ingeniously, the lower section is subtly showcasing her Midwestern charm. When she reaches out for a book, a tantalizing hint of her underboob is captured by an onlooker, presenting an intriguing contrast to the academic surroundings. At first glance, who would have anticipated such a cozy outfit could project such a sex appeal? As she moves, a keen observer might notice her bold choice to forgo a bra, a fact concealed by the string knit which, while not revealing outright, leaves a haunting impression on those who watch her for a more extended period. This unexpected yet subtly provocative nuance sets her apart. She is not just any library dweller; she personifies the essence of "Library Hot."

Parallel: The "Hot Library" style presents an intriguing parallel with academic aesthetics, but it's more than just that. It weaves in a touch of playful naughtiness into the traditionally austere academic look. This style moves beyond the stereotypical headband and pleated skirt.

Youth Option: The youthful interpretation of this style is a vibrant celebration of both the glitz of innocent youth as It channels the vitality of school days while acknowledging the style element evolution that comes with age. This look serves as a visual narration of your journey of self-discovery and the unveiling of your feminine allure. The deft blending of juvenile and mature elements creates an irresistible look.

Mature Option: As for the mature woman, this style remains a perfect fit. The playful details like ribbons and long white socks, suggestive of youthful exuberance, may be omitted. But you can lean into the knitted outfits that exude a sensual touch, like off off-shoulder dress or a skirt and jacket set like I mentioned in the envision part. The beauty of this style lies in its versatility—you have the liberty to choose what to keep and what to leave.

Occasion: The smart woman's choice, perfect for obvious academic activities like study-oriented dates, when you choose to put your study buddy under a seductive spell. It can even become your everyday go-to attire if you wish. Just be careful, okay?

Recipe

1. **Staples:** The foundation of your wardrobe should be built on classic staples: an elegantly pleated skirt, wool or cashmere sweaters and cardigans, tweed sets, a tight knitted vest, a neatly tailored white blouse, and structured blazers.

2. **Oomph:** Keep in mind, that you still need to make it hot, so if you are wearing a blazer, a mini skirt is a must. If your choice is a loose cashmere sweater, then slipped-off shoulder detail would be the must. If it is a cotton dress, combine it with sexy bold boots.

3. **Teasing with Details:** An eye-catching statement headband or hair bow can serve as a whimsical yet stylish addition, adding a dash of playfulness. Glasses are the ultimate smart-sexy move. Or when you choose the right pair of glasses, they can frame your face attractively, adding an intellectual charm.

4. **Combinations:** Picture the indulgent warmth of wool, its plush texture seemingly made for those cool library nights, turning them into intoxicating moments. Imagine a cozy sweater, draped suggestively off one shoulder, whispering tales of sensuality as you lose yourself in a riveting novel. The quintessential tweed, its intellectual charm fused with a bold. Visualize an enticing tweed ensemble - a demure jacket paired with a daringly short skirt. Choose to add long socks or high boots, and you've got an irresistible look that sizzles. Cotton, with its innocent simplicity, seduces you, offering breathability and comfort. Envision a soft, casual mini dress for the summer, combined with audacious boots and a scholarly jacket, all crafted from this modest yet seductive fabric. And let's not forget the irresistible pull of dreamy cashmere ensembles.

Red Hot Details

The Allure of Knee-high Socks: Knee-high socks are more than just an accessory – they are the symbol of seduction. Straddling the line between playfulness and seduction, these fashion staples imbue the wearer with an aura of youthful charm. Remember, confidence is key – let your knee-highs be a bold testament to your individuality and fashion prowess.

It's All About that Extra Mini Skirt: The extra mini skirt is the epitome of cheeky academic allure. It's a daring, statement piece that screams confidence and flirty fun. Whether paired with a snug turtleneck or an oversized blazer, the extra mini skirt always takes center stage. It's the embodiment of academic freedom, a stand against the mundane, and a celebration of the vibrant, dynamic nature of the wearer.

Strut in Knee-high Boots: Nothing quite encapsulates the "Hot Library" as those knee-high boots. From glossy, black leather to soft, supple suede, these boots exude a sense of powerful femininity. They're the perfect complement to a cozy sweater dress or a plaid skirt. Knee-high boots are about making a statement, about stepping with authority and assurance, and bonus points if your heel is sturdy, just like your knowledge about being hot.

Let the teasing begin,
all credit to being smart.

Inspiration

Temptress Features

In the following pages, you will find instructions on how to create alluring features. You can choose one or all of them. I have personally tried each look, and each one of them guaranteed me compliments.

The "Angelic Hair"

#tightly-waved-hair

Ready To Be Enchanted? Use this hairstyle that's pure celestial magic!

First Things First: Long, luscious locks are your ticket to this ethereal look. But there is no harm in working with what you have.

Creating a Buzz!: Have you heard saying "The outfit is my hair today?" It is the same case with "Angelic Hair". Every time I've styled my hair into this look, the whirlwind of compliments and admiring glances has been almost overwhelming. It's like having a radiant aura surrounding your hair that simply captivates anybody who looks at you. And while I'm not entirely sure of its spellbinding secret, one thing's for sure: it's heavenly. So, I fondly named it "Angelic Hair" since it's part of the earlier mentioned angelic look.

The Spotlight's on You, Darling: Feeling like you're walking under a soft spotlight? That's the charm of this style! Just remember, let the hair be the star, over-powering makeup is a crime with it. Choose outfits like a Grecian one-shoulder gown or a simple cut-fitted outfit if you want to look elegant. If you aim to project a welcoming and flirtatious demeanor, consider adopting touch of "Fairy Girl" aesthetic. This style, characterized by its softly playful and pastel-hued color palette, effectively communicates femininity and approachability.

Your Outfit, Your Canvas: While there's a special kind of magic in long blonde tresses with this style, know that it dazzles with any shade. In my days of flaunting extra-long hair in this style, I felt like I was walking my own catwalk. And trust me, the world noticed. You can have this magic, too!

Occasion: Perfect for owning the urban jungle or casting a spell during romantic seaside evenings. Though, Darling, perhaps it's best to leave this particular look out of the boardroom; it might just be a touch too flirtatious for a formal setting.

Recipe

The No-Heat Glam-Up:

1. **Freshen up, Gorgeous:** Hit the shower for squeaky-clean tresses.

2. **Almost There:** Blow dry just until your locks feel temptingly damp.

3. **Elevate that Volume:** Slather on some volume mousse magic from root to tip.

4. **French Braid Fiesta:** Weave those locks into an elegant French braid, letting them marinate either overnight or for a cool two-hour minimum.

5. **Unleash the Curls:** Gently unravel your braids, letting your fingers do the styling.

6. **The Final Glow-Up:** Add a dollop of hair oil for that divine shimmer.

Recipe

The Heat-Styled Stunner:

1. **Let's Get it Started:** Cleanse that beautiful mane. Maybe even use a vinegar-infused conditioner for that extra shine.

2. **Shine Time:** Mist on some heat protectant spray for that extra glam.

3. **Go Sleek or Go Curly:** Now it's time to Blow dry until smooth and straight.

4. **Mermaid Vibes Ahead:** Craft those killer waves with the 3/4-barrel mermaid hair tool.

Shoutout: I could never forget about my naturally curly Beauty; you get a special shoutout. Every day is an angelic day for you. Simply separate and smooth those luscious locks into a reflective halo; you were born already as an ethereal queen.

There you have it, my stunning Siren! You're now fully equipped to flaunt your "Angelic Magic."

The "M Lined Lips"

#cupids-bow-lips

Use Cupid's bow as your magic wand, casting a spell of enchantment over your chosen one.

The Little Black Dress of Lips: Ah, the "M Lined" lips – they are like the little black dress of the makeup world. Have you ever received compliments for a pronounced cupid's bow in the past? Feels great, right?

Cupid Shot: This graceful shape echoes the very bow used by Cupid, the mythical god of desire and affection in Roman mythology. As the tale goes, Cupid would draw his bow and let loose arrows imbued with love, piercing the hearts of unsuspecting mortals and deities alike. The subtle curve and dip of the "M" Lined lips evoke this ancient symbol of romance, adding an ethereal touch to a woman's smile.

A Kiss From a Rose: Indeed, an iconic letter stamped with a kiss would be imprinted with a scarlet red "M" lined lip.

The Secret: Gorgeous, the key is to fully own your one-of-a-kind allure. Whether your lips are sculpted like a love-struck Cupid's bow or boast a distinctive round silhouette that's exclusively yours, be your masterpiece, a living work of art that captivates and enchants just by being unapologetically you.

Go With the Flow: Embracing the "M Lip Lining" technique means tracing the natural silhouette of your lips. It's all about employing a deeper lipliner hue while highlighting the center with a softer shade, making your natural lip contours and cupid's bow take center stage.

Unique Allure: Many iconic beauties of our era, who are effortlessly elegant and widely admired, proudly exhibit this "M" shape. I bet you can already imagine a few!

Recipe ✏

1. **Indulge in a Velvety Start:** Opt for a gentle lip scrub to unveil a luscious canvas.

2. **Define with Elegance:** Conceal around those lips, carving a pathway to the allure. For excess concealer on the inner parts of your lips, consider using a slightly damp Q-tip to gently remove any surplus product.

3. **Time to Glow, Gorgeous:** Lightly grace your cupid's bow with a touch of celestial highlighter. Alternatively, you may choose to incorporate the highlighter during the previous step by blending a few drops into your concealer.

4. **Paint an "X" of Enchantment:** Utilize your cupid's bow as a reference, and with a lipliner, sketch an "X" so that the pinnacle of the "X" corresponds to the apex of your cupid's bow. This method guarantees a harmonious and even distribution of your lip product.

5. **Silhouette:** Trace your lips capturing their essence with the liner's elegant sweep.

6. **Mix a Magic Potion:** Fill the core of your lips with two shades of lighter lipstick, letting them waltz together.

7. **The Finishing Touch?:** A flirtatious dab of blush at the heart of your bottom lip, and top it off with lip balm.

"Cat-Curve" Brows

#perfect-arched-brows

Feline wildness with a touch of grace,
adding mystery to your face.

Memory Lane:

This unique style first sparked my interest thanks to one of my closest friends (shoutout to a twenty-one-year friendship mark). Her allure was undeniably feminine and captivating, yet she achieved this without succumbing to the typical trappings of a girlish world. Her beauty routine was simple, often limited to a tint of moisturizer, a dash of eyeliner, and a generous coat of mascara. It would be apt to describe her as a carefree, sporty young woman. I, on the other hand, was the polar opposite. I reveled in the charm of makeup and never shied away from trying new beauty routines. One might call me a makeup maven, while she was more of a racing track diva.

The "Aha!" Moment: One day, I accompanied her to a karting competition, playing the role of her supportive friend and watching her race with the boys. The moment she emerged from her kart and up-lifted her helmet shield, I had an epiphany. And then it clicked for me—her beauty, it was all in those dramatic, feline brows! It was the secret to her enigmatic allure, even without layers of foundation and contour. They were perfectly curved, giving her the air of a cat-like siren, fresh from the race. A simple yet transformative detail that turned my dearest friend into a magnetic vixen, effortlessly capturing attention.

Naturally: I had to give it a go. When something looks that alluring, you've got to try it yourself. Imitation is a form of flattery! So, since she had this stunning feline look without any other makeup help, I named them the "Cat-Curve Brows."

Up For It?: This eyebrow artistry is a rare gem. This is one shape that may take a lot of practice, but *wow,* is it worth it, given how mesmerizing it looks, that just exudes the vibe of a Cat-woman. This isn't just a look; it's a vibe, a statement, a declaration of your feline mystique. Me-ow!

The Magic Touch: Given my fine, delicate brow hairs, I need to put in time and effort to perfect it. You need perfect symmetry, high-quality grooming, gel, and your most trusted brow tools, but believe me, the results are pure magic. It might not be every face's unique shape, but there's no harm in trying and seeing for yourself.

Why It's so Feminine: These brows serve the task of accentuating femininity, the impact is undeniable. You might ask, how I be so certain? Consider this - if a man were to adopt this particular brow shape, he would radiate a confusingly feminine allure.

Perfection: Whenever I embrace this style or paint it on my friends, it's as if their faces undergo a mesmerizing transformation. It's what I lovingly call "Face-Feminization," an artful metamorphosis that takes you from everyday glam to a feline goddess. It's as if your face becomes a canvas for a captivating tale of allure and mystique. Simply put, it's perfection.

Occasion: It's a lifestyle choice, Gorgeous! Whether you're leading an iconic life or planning to seduce someone special over a romantic dinner, cat-curve brows will be your magic wand.

Recipe

1. **Big Bush:** You want to have a nice bush to start with, so perhaps using castor oil could benefit you, at least it did for me.

2. **Time for a Scrub:** Gently exfoliate those brows; as any artist starts with your canvas being clean.

3. **Map Your Brow's High Point:** Look no further than the outer edge of your iris – that's where your brow should have a fabulous curve. Follow the shape using tweezers. Let the start of your brow (next to your nose) be bigger, and after the curve, it gets slimmer.

4. **Ready for a Lift:** Apply gel to the start of your brow, combing upwards. If that's not enough for you, use an eyebrow lamination kit for the starting part of the brow.

5. **Tidy Up:** Don't be shy to trim those wild ones, so they align in a straight, show-stopping line.

6. **Let's add Some Drama, Darling:** Elevate your brows to their full diva potential by sweeping on some brow mascara—sensational glam in a simple tube.

7. **And the Grand Brow Finish:** Craft that brow tail to be sleek, smooth, and as sharp as your wit.

Visual Recipe

Wink with confidence and brow beauty. You're ready to mesmerize!

The "Bed Hair" Allure

Nostalgia Alert!: Okay, so "Bed Hair?" Yup, you've definitely heard of this look before flipping through this book. Flashback to the late '90s and early 2000s – think of that iconic messy, hot girl beach blonde we all had a little love for. Yeah, you know who I'm talking about!

Memory Lane:

Transformation: Ever since I saw the iconic beach blonde sprinting along the shoreline in her red swimsuit, I was captivated by her iconic hair. Unfortunately, my hair was naturally straight, long, and with a straight cut. So I was never able to do the iconic "Bed Hair", until last year when I underwent a complete 180-degree transformation pulling the "Cleopatra Effect. " I dyed my hair beach blonde and completed the look with extensions, which added fantastic layers to my hair. Now I was ready to replicate the iconic hairstyle I'd always admired. After numerous trials, I finally mastered the perfect technique.

Iconic Feeling: The moment of truth came during a beach club lunch reservation with my boyfriend. Dressed in a minimalist silk mini dress and nude sandals, my hair was styled into intentionally tousled, voluminous locks - the iconic "Bed Hair." As I expected, the impact was significant. My boyfriend was so awestruck by my transformation; that he could barely eat. His compliment – "This must be the sexiest I have ever seen you"– was quite jarring. However, it made me realize how transformative the power of hair can be. After all, my outfit was simple - no push-ups or anything otherwise sexy, just a silk dress and modest sandals. Yet, it was my hairstyle that truly amplified my allure.

What Makes it HOT: Why does the "Bad Hair" look hold an irresistible appeal? You must Imagine the light catching perfectly imperfect layers, each strand contributing to a compelling narrative of wild allure and confident sexiness. This "Bed Hair" style is making it seem as though you've just stepped out of an intoxicating whirlwind romance. Hair that whispers tales of untamed passion. There is something thrillingly magnetic about this narrative, weaving a spell of wild magic. So why not seize the moment?

To Bun, or Not to Bun?: Now, you can rock this look up in a messy bun or let it flow down, wild and free. But heads up, arling: layers in your hair are important to this look. Without a few choppy but styled layers, it might not achieve full effect, but anyway, it's worth trying.

Occasion: This hairstyle is perfect for a flirty day. Keep in mind that, it might not vibe with your 9-to-5 look. Save it for those wild nights out or lazy brunch dates. Note: Keep the hairstyle away from your Monday's boardroom meeting.

Recipe

1. **Time for a Splash:** Wash that gorgeous mane.

2. **Go Big or Go Home:** Apply volume mousse from the roots all the way down.

3. **Remember, it's all About the VOLUME:** Blow dry upside down and embrace the chaos. Not lioness enough after the blow dry? Girl, amp it up! Add some root lifting powder spray or dab in extra mousse.

4. **Rock Those Big Hot Rollers:** The bigger, the better.

5. **After the Grand Roller Reveal:** Flip the hair down and run your fingers through it for that effortless tousle.

6. **Optional:** Spritz a bit of texture spray. But Honey, don't go overboard; we want breezy and carefree, not sticky and hard hair.

7. **Updo Option:** With a handful of your hair, create an enchanting twist. Using French pins. Start by inserting 5 to 10 of these magic makers into the twisted tresses to create a hold. It's the perfect blend of chaos and cuteness. Allow a few strands to escape from your updo. Let them flow freely, gracefully contouring your face and framing your features. Maybe give them an extra swirl with a curling iron.

Embrace your wild side and let your "Bed Hair" become the star.

"Hollywood Neck" Exposure

Ready to unleash that sultry exposure? Let's sculpt you into a Hollywood temptress!

Hollywood Hair: Alright, Gorgeous, ever heard of that sizzling Hollywood hairstyle? It's the whole "Mysterious on one side, total flirt on the other" vibe. luscious waves effortlessly cascading down one side while the other side unveils your neck—bare, inviting, and alluring.

Magnetic Pull: Doing the "Hollywood Neck" isn't just about hair. It's about staging a magnetic pull where one side of your hair acts like a protective curtain (if you're blessed with Rapunzel-like locks) while the other unveils that oh-so-kissable neck. In real-life intimate moments, the neck has a way of drawing your partner in like a siren's call, and it's no mystery why—it's an undeniable erogenous zone.

The Primal Dance: Unveiling the psychology behind exposing one's neck takes us back to our primal roots. The neck, a vulnerable treasure trove housing vital arteries and the trachea, becomes an emblem of trust and submission when revealed. This is not a sign of weakness but a delicate display of openness, a non-threatening signal that fosters intimate connections and piques attraction. It holds the power of vulnerability, but there's more to this neck revelation.

The Strength Affirmation: It's also a testament to courage and power, a declaration that you are unafraid to expose your most susceptible area. This intriguing mix of vulnerability and audacity adds a layer to its irresistible charm, enhancing the magnetic pull.

Occasion: Timeless & Limitless! While you can absolutely serve this look whenever the mood strikes, it truly shines in the softer, more intimate settings. Think candlelit dinner dates or romantic evenings where you're aiming for that deep, soulful connection. It's an entire vibe designed to captivate.

Recipe

1. **Catch the Wave:** Start by giving your hair those enviable, bougie Hollywood-inspired waves.

2. **Time for Your Star Moment:** Sweep your luxurious mane to one side as if you're the star of a high-end shampoo commercial.

3. **Now, Let's Carve Art:** Add a touch of contour to your collarbone to give it that irresistible depth.

4. **Pop, Lock, and Shine:** Dazzle those collarbones with a hit of highlighter. Yes, make them a showstopper!

5. **Wait, there's More?:** Oh, absolutely! Glide some highlighter over those shoulders for an extra dash of glam.

6. **Scent-Sational Finish:** Spritz some sexy perfume on the neck's pull point.

7. **A little Pro Tip:** If you're hoping for a kiss, keep the perfume behind your ears so it smells divine without leaving a bitter taste on your neck.

The "Collarbone Effect"

Ready to mesmerize with every glance and gesture? Let's dial up your seductive elegance to a new level!

Memory Lane:

Star Power: Oh, the collarbone – also known as the "Beauty Bone." I remember, back in the day when I was working as a model in Milan. The photographers were simply obsessed with taking pictures that highlighted the sweeping drama of the collarbone. That's when it clicked—this beauty bone had star power. I realized "That Girl" had nice collarbones. It's an elegant sweep at the base of our neck? Pure magic.

One Size Does Not Fit All: Now, if your collarbone's playing hide-and-seek, Girl, no stress. Maybe contouring's the way to go. Or, hey, on the next page, there I'm revealing perhaps a more fitting fabulous trick for You. As they say, one shoe size will not fit all—whether your collarbones are popping or hiding, the glam world's got room for all. Each of us has our unique fabulousness.

Your Built-In Bling: Think of collarbones as built-in necklaces just beneath the skin. They bring that *oomph* to your neckline. So, if you're feeling sassy, flaunt them in an outfit that lets them shine.

What Makes it HOT: The Dance of Shadows by Collarbones. Their subtle prominence traces a delicate arc, creating a natural stage where light and shadow perform an enticing dance, as it adds alluring depth to your appearance. So, ladies, embrace the seductive charm of your collarbones.

Occasion: Sunshine & Starlight! This look is your go-to for those golden summer days when you're glowing from head to toe. But don't put it away when the sun sets—collarbones can be irresistible in Moonlight as well - if you know what I mean.

Recipe

1. **Prepare Your Canvas:** Start with perhaps an enzyme cleanser followed by moisturizer on your décolleté area. Once it's done it should radiate a sheer glow finish.

2. **Still Dull?:** Add some tinted glowing foundation. To achieve a more sheer finish, you can mix it with your moisturizer.

3. **Get Ready for Collarbone Couture:** Sculpt them with a dash of contour to elevate the contrast dance. Where naturally shadow would fall you use a darker contour stick, but at the higher points, you accent them with concealer.

4. **Sparkle Alert:** Dab that highlighter on the high points— yes, Gorgeous, that's where you become an ethereal vision. Don't forget the shoulders.

5. **The Cherry on Top:** Buy a little chain that hangs the same length as your collarbones and add a little pendant that falls in the hole where they meet. This will accent the part so much more. I call it the collarbone necklace hack. It's so sexy and alluring.

Décolletage "Show Time"

Get ready to unlock their bosom potential. It's "Girls"' showtime!

Embrace Your Uniqueness: Gorgeous, it's time to acknowledge that we're like snowflakes—unique and beautiful. We don't all come with the same curves; our bosoms are as individual as our fingerprints. This chapter is all about celebrating your unique "Girls." Here, you'll discover the ultimate showstopper tips tailored to highlight your unique chest type so you can flaunt their captivating charm to the fullest. These suggestions contain one of each. Look at it as a starting point for your "Girls" parade that can inspire you to pay attention to them in the way "They" like.

Athletic (Wide-muscular-less-tissue)

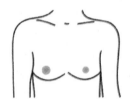 

The Allure of Athletic Appeal: Showcasing one's athletic chest goes hand in hand with donning tops that snugly cinch at the center, giving them a little squeeze. You see, when there's less fluff and more firmness—a testament to your hard-earned muscle—a top that wraps around snugly helps bring those muscles to the forefront. And a touch of squeezing? Well, that's just the cherry on top to squeeze that "Juicy" appeal out.

Slender (Thin-nipples-go-down)

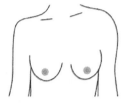 

Dainty and Downwards?: If you're graced with petite charms or your assets naturally favor the downward gaze, I have a hack for you. Opt for ensembles endowed with a tantalizing texture and voluminous verve, like this delightful number illustrated. Its skillful design paints the illusion of a fuller, perkier silhouette, inviting a renewed sense of bouncy allure. So, doll up and let your breasts feel that irresistible lift.

Bell (Slimmer-top-fuller-bottom)

Enchanting Chimes: Here's a styling tip for all you lovely ladies graced with the bell-like bust shape. Consider treating yourself to balcony bra-tops that have been made out of strong "Bones" that bring them together in a tight and firm manner. If you have larger breasts, the bigger the underband the safer the hold. This unique design offers the perfect fit while holding them strong in place and enhancing your natural allure. To sprinkle some extra charm, add a dash of lace overlay to the mix.

Left-Right (Nipples-point-opposite)

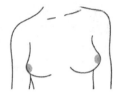 

Wandering Wonders, Meet Straight Necklines: If your generous assets have a penchant for casting glances in divergent directions, consider a low, straight, but tight neckline for your next ensemble. Your breasts will appear larger since they extend out on the sides of your body. The straight neckline creates the illusion of fullness in the center, and your nipples work like pillars for the illusion.

Relaxed (Soft-tissue-points-down)

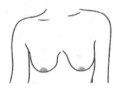 

The Laid-Back Luxe: The relaxed bust shape is one of the most popular ones, particularly post-maternity. Now, let's unveil the secret to enhance this natural beauty. Opt for a thick material garment that holds its own shape. The main star of the show? Adorn the middle with a captivating accent, perhaps a delicate rose or a charming symbol of femininity. But if you feel like they are hanging too low- look for a garment that offers support with straps. You'll be amazed at how exquisite they appear!

Side Set (wide-space-between)

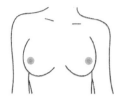 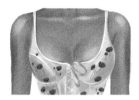

Reunion by Corsetry, My Dears: If your distinct assets prefer their own spaces, fear not. Contemplate a rendezvous through the art of corsetry. This stunning piece of garment, known for its cinching magic, gently persuades your gifts to reconvene at a harmonious midpoint. So, let the classic charm of a corset bridge the gap, redefining your silhouette with an elegant unity.

Round (Full-top-full-bottom)

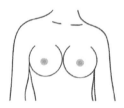 

The Divine Delight of Rounded Wonders: Dear curvaceous Goddess, isn't it a divine delight to be the chosen bearer of such rounded paradises? You, my love, can do justice to any garment with an effortless grace. If you're ready to fully embrace and flaunt your natural allure, your endowed beauty is ideal for the task. Opting for a deep V neckline, just like the iconic "Bond Girl" does, it will render the spectators utterly speechless.

Teardrop (Round-slightly-slender-top)

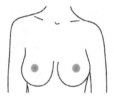 

Dreamy Teardrop: Uff, Dear, the teardrop shape, is so dreamy. The triangled-shaped apparel is the way to go! You see, it mirrors the very essence of your bosom, gracefully transitioning from lesser volume at the top to a fuller, more voluptuous base, akin to a triangle expanding from a slender tip to a wider bottom. So, why not pair these two into the toxic cocktail?

You found your shape, but your girls are extra petite?

High Fashion Hot: your unique beauty lies in the flirtatious charm you effortlessly exude. Having little breasts can give you a chance to wear the most risqué garments, keeping you looking sexy in a very classy way. It's the high fashion hotness. Accent your petite treasures through the playful tease of pearl stripes, and embellishments on your garment around the cleavage, maybe the way to go is the seductive whisper of lace. As long as you maintain that flirtatious spirit, your elegance will continue to dazzle. Embrace your petite perfection.

The Seducing Moves

Strength is key, and posture is a must.

The Fundamentals

She Knows the Moves: Gorgeous, I have some tantalizing moves up my sleeve that have proven their efficiency wonders over and over. So why wouldn't they work for you, too? They're sure to be the perfect cherry on top of the irresistible game of seduction you might soon be playing. But not so fast. Before we start, let's go over the basics coz you can't build a home without the foundations. You may think these are things you already know, but you won't be able to fully take advantage of the techniques if these basics are not in check. So, let's begin, shall we?

You Got Your Own Back: Remember, always maintain a straight back. This posture not only exudes confidence but also enhances the appearance of your "Girls," making them appear more prominent.

Shoulder Art: Your shoulders should be relaxed and poised but never hunched. Them being hunched might give an impression of "guessing why you are in this room, rather than owning it," and we don't want that, do we?

Chin Your Way Up: Lastly, be mindful of the "Phone Chin;" extend your neck gracefully. If you must look down, do it with a straight neck.

Seductive "S" Pose

#standing-in-letter-s-shape

Goddess Sculpture: This deeply feminine posture, my Dears, is reminiscent of a beautifully crafted painting or a sculpture of a Greek goddess. You're not merely standing; you're a living, breathing work of art.

Picture This: You're poised at a lounge bar, anticipation bubbling within you as your dirty martini is in the works. You're swathed in a breathtakingly snug dress that showcases your alluring figure. Eyes from across the room are magnetically drawn to you, taking in your stunning ensemble. Here's where the "S" stance comes into play. You're going to adopt this sultry "S" shape.

Recipe✒

1. **The Graceful Dip:** Initiate the move with your hips, gracefully dipping into one side. This is the starting point of your "S" pose journey.

2. **Leg Crossover:** The leg on the side of the dipped hip? Cross it over the other, adding a flirtatious twist to your stance. You're already halfway there!

3. **Core Engagement:** Now, let your core join the rhythm, adding a subtle yet sultry curve to your silhouette. Feel your body flowing with the rhythm.

4. **The Natural Fall:** Time for your arms to join the party. Allow them to fall naturally, relaxed, and effortlessly. Feel the ease and grace of your pose.

5. **Chic Bar Lean:** Maybe it's time to elevate your "S" pose by one elbow casually taking the support delicately leaning against the bar or resting on the side of your upper hip. Relish the whole vibe of your "S" stance.

The "Determining Smile"

#flirting-using-silence

Game-Changer: I've got you covered with a fabulous trick to reclaim the reins in your tango of interaction.

Imagine This: You're out on a date; perhaps it's time for a touch of playful flirtation, or maybe the conversation seems to be dwindling, and nerves are creeping in. Never fear. I've got you! When your moment to reply arrives, you'll bypass the ordinary response, and instead, you'll embark on this splendid tactic:

Recipe

1. **Shh...:** Embrace a silent moment.

2. **Shoulder Confidence:** pull your shoulders back, assuming a confident posture. Be ready to command the silent play.

3. **Inquisitive Tilt and Play:** Now, subtly lower your head a bit and angle it in one direction, then shift your eyes toward the side opposite to where you've inclined your head. As if pondering something perplexing yet intriguing. Remember, subtlety is key. If you have a cocktail, bring it to your lips and enjoy a sip. If not, engage in some playful hair-touching.

4. **Assertive Glance:** Next, cast an assured and slightly aloof gaze toward them, combining it with a hint of a smile. Let them get nervous and wonder what's on your mind.

5. **Silent Flirt Tensity:** This silence is your secret weapon, creating a palpable flirtatious tension. You've just soared to new heights in your flirt dynamics.

6. **The Bonus:** Here's a bonus tip for the shy ones—you've just gotten them talking again without uttering a single word. Marvel at the power of non-verbal communication.

The "Cartoon Cat Swing"

#swinging-hips-walk

Feline Walk: Make your moves a form of art, and who to take it from. The best example of the exaggeration of the perfect feminine movements is a cartoon cat. I'm sure it already comes to your mind: the way female cats used to move in cartoons in a flirtatious way. Even though they were cats, you could capture the femininity flowing out of them, and you knew they were about to get their way. So why not apply it to your movements and swing those feminine curves?

Recipe✓

1. **Hip Leadership:** Initiate each stride by slightly advancing your hips, allowing them to guide your movement. This posture illuminates your self-assuredness.

2. **Rhythm Discovery:** Tune in to your unique rhythm, letting your hips sway naturally with each step. Imagine you have a tail that you are trying to swing a bit (don't go overboard). This will display your comfort and harmony within your body.

3. **Graceful Tempo:** Infuse your movements with a touch of delicate slowness, creating a dance-like cadence with each step. This shows, that you are relaxed and enjoying your day and what can be more sexy than that?

4. **Confidence Exuding:** Every stride is a statement of confidence that illustrates your acceptance and love for your body. Revel in the power of self-assured body language.

5. **Soft Hand Ballet:** When you're about to touch or pick up something, think of it as a ballet. Slowly and gracefully gesture your arms toward objects (don't go overboard).

The "Sirens Call" at the Bar

#flirting-with-your-eyes

Capturing Attention: The simplest and most alluring method to kindle a spark with someone you find appealing is through the power of your gaze.

Picture the Scene: You're at a bar, and there's someone nearby who you find attractive, and wish that the person would approach you. It's your moment to deliver a captivating "Siren's Call" with your eyes- specific eye contact:

Recipe

1. **Sidelong Glance:** If shyness is a part of your charm, fear not. Casually notice their presence through the corners of your eyes. This soft approach can make you feel more comfortable.

2. **Purposeful Stare:** Ensure your gaze communicates that this is no accidental fleeting look, but rather, a deliberate engagement. Wait until they look back at you, and then count to four before looking away.

3. **Eyes' Allure Amplified:** Always remember, your eyes are an expressive powerhouse. Intensifying their charm using makeup can magnetize the power of your gaze.

4. **Flirtatious Touch:** Introduce an extra dose of flirtation by subtly lowering your head, then raising your gaze and gently fluttering your lashes.

5. **Mastering Smizing:** Pair your flirtatious look with the art of "smizing, " a term that combines smiling with your eyes. It radiates warmth and friendliness through your eyes. When you successfully smile, your eyes appear to sparkle, while your facial expressions remain relaxed.

"Women are Players Too"

#playful-touch-with-hands

Prepare the Playing Instrument: An essential prerequisite of this game is having your primary tool prepared, namely, your hands. Their charm can shape the destiny of your flirtatious endeavors, weaving a mesmerizing spell over your admirer. After all, the more feminine and aesthetically pleasing they are, the more fruitful the results are likely to be.

Recipe

The Temptatious Appeal:

6. **Manicure:** Enhance the allure of your hands by maintaining a neat manicure, preferably with almond, coffin, or stiletto-shaped nails which are often perceived as attractive and extra feminine shape. If your hands are very feminine you can easily go with short squared shapes as well. When you think about colors, classic ones always will have your back and will give you the highest success rate. Those include nudes, pinks, French manicures, and red nails.

7. **Bracelets:** Accessorizing can make your hands look more appealing and playful. For the highest success rate: opt for denty bracelets, in gold or silver colors, they can have some crystals or gemstones in them. Stay away from ones that are extra bulky, and made out of cheap-looking strings.

8. **Playful Hands:** Enhance the beauty of your fingers with tastefully selected rings that exude charm, and femineity. One to three rings is enough. So, be cautious not to overload your fingers with bulky rings that could give off an unintended impression of a pirate or fortune-teller. Remember, hands should exude a comforting aura rather than a daunting one… if you're looking to seduce.

All Set: Now that your hands are primed and poised for action, we can now delve into the incredible world of the flirtation game. Prepare for a comprehensive guide on touch, and let the dance of seduction begin.

Recipe

The Player movements:

1. **Necklace Flirt:** This approach calls for a necklace or a lower neckline. As part of your flirtatious repertoire. The idea here is to delicately toy with your necklace, letting it dance between your fingertips sliding it back and forth. Or sliding your fingertips over your collarbone. This not only draws the viewer's attention to your neck and collarbone area, an undeniable symbol of sensuality but also adds a flirty, playful tone to your interaction. It's a non-verbal way of saying, "I've got your attention now, haven't I?"

2. **Slide on Them:** Amidst a lively conversation, when you respond with heightened enthusiasm, you might consider incorporating a subtle touch. It could be a light stroke of your hand on his/her upper leg, or gently resting your hand on theirs. A brief caress on the arm or leg can serve as a suggestive signal, while a touch to the shoulder might resonate more as a friendly "Bro Gesture." Always remember, that the power of touch can be a magnetic moment.

3. **The Face-Touch Gesture:** A subtle touch on your face or lips can send a potent signal. This gesture, when combined with a well-manicured hand, can emit a seductive aura that captures and holds the other person's attention. It's a non-verbal way of saying, "Are you captivated yet?"

Flirtation "Dos and Don'ts"

Engaging With an Admirer: Gorgeous, listen up! Amidst the lively thrum of social gatherings, exude an air of confidence as you allow the admirer to lean into your sphere for a conversation. However, if you detect a role reversal, with you leaning in, it might be time to take a flirtatious step back. This could hint at a waning interest in the other party and may portray you as someone not being in receiving energy aka feminine energy. Remember, you're playing a tantalizing game of attraction!

Overt Palms: Open your palms; let them be seen. Showcasing your palms acts as a silent proclamation of your sincerity, signaling that you have nothing to conceal. This subtle gesture can contribute to establishing an atmosphere of trust and safety.

Avoiding Crossed Arms: Refrain from crossing your arms as it is a universal sign of defensiveness and disinterest. This protective stance could deter the lively exchange of flirtatious energy, and could inadvertently send signals of you not being open to the interaction. Remember to maintain an inviting demeanor, echoing the fluid dance of flirtation.

Shying Away: Shunning eye contact may leave you appearing distant or uninterested, potentially dimming the spark of attraction. Although balance is the key, so don't turn it into a staring contest either.

"You Know…She Knows" Approved Aphrodisiacs.

"Use with precaution, concentrated."

Aphrodisiacal Clothing

The second skin you wore, so light and sheer, a memory cherished, year after year.

Sartorial Elixirs: Here is the "Essence Oil" in its raw form from the viewpoint of a **"You Know...She Knows"** approved aphrodisiac—a potent substance to wield with caution. Seduction it's a delicate art. And remember, with essences, you can get burned. They are very powerful, so use them wisely and at the right moments. Or if your intention is literally to set someone on fire, add more of the amount.

Fabric:

Starting Point: The adventure initiates with fabrics. Undeniably, fabrics can either emit an enticing aura or the exact opposite. Knowing how to mix in these essences of clothing can elevate your sex appeal in no time.

- **Satin Finish**: The silky dream holds an intrinsic allure due to its smoothness, luxurious feel, and the soft sheen it exudes. Its unique texture and appearance have a way of catching and reflecting light, creating visual stimulation that stirs a sensual intrigue, making it a perfect choice for clothing aimed at enhancing feminine charm. The way satin drapes and flows can also accentuate the body's natural curves, adding to its seductive potential.

- **Lace:** The siren of fabrics inherently exudes an allure that's both delicate and provocative. It's the juxtaposition of its intricate patterns, simultaneously revealing and concealing skin, that fuels its sensuous charm. Lace has a long-standing association with femininity and romance, making it a potent ingredient in the recipe for seductive attire. This explains why Lace is the reigning queen in the kingdom of sexy lingerie. Whether used as an accent to a garment or as the main fabric, lace adds a layer of intrigue and allure.

- **Tulle or Chiffon:** Also known as transparent mesh fabric, it is an exquisite embodiment of tantalizing allure and sophisticated subterfuge. It exudes an allure that's both ethereal and provocative. Its sheer transparency, coupled with a seductive color, can transform even the simplest outfit into an irresistible siren call. When paired with a lacy bra underneath, an elegant see-through blouse can stir a captivating curiosity, teasing the onlooker. It's this playful interplay of veiling and unveiling that lends this fabric its seductive potential.

- **Leather:** An embodiment of intoxicating authority and dominatrix energy. Its texture, simultaneously sleek and rugged, captivates the eye, while its undeniable toughness introduces an element of audacity and daring. Whether it's a tight-fit skirt, a pair of gloves, or a daring harness, leather possesses an inimitable allure that is both powerful and tantalizing. Its ability to fit closely to the body's shape highlights the wearer's silhouette, while its tactile allure triggers a myriad of sensations.

- **Cashmere:** This premium fabric may not be the first that comes to mind when considering enticing materials, yet it possesses a unique allure. The appeal of cashmere lies not so much in its visual presentation but rather in the tactile experience it offers. Imagine donning a snug, off-the-shoulder cashmere dress. The inviting softness of the fabric captures your partner's interest, while the hand traces its path along the material. The sumptuous sensation of touching cashmere, akin to a celestial encounter, triggers a subconscious association of this pleasant experience with your personal allure

Aphrodisiac Color Palette:

Impact Play: As we continue to navigate our way through the art of seductive appeal, we shouldn't underestimate the impact of the color palette. Specific shades have an innate ability to evoke feelings and draw the eye more effectively than others. These bewitching hues, ladies, serve as your color-coded love potions, subtly infusing your attire and amplifying your captivating allure.

- **Rubi Red:** Often associated with love and passion, is a color that exudes confidence, power, and allure. Its vibrant hue captures attention and holds it, making it a go-to color for those seeking to make a bold and sexy statement.

Perfect for: An evening dress, intimate lingerie, a sirens sweater, or as a bold accent color for nails, lips, boots, and bags.

- **Emerald Green:** This magnificent shade of green exudes an aura of royalty. Known for its soothing properties, the color green imparts a sense of relaxation. Thus, attiring yourself in emerald green not only radiates regal vibes but also creates a calming and serene atmosphere for those in your company.

Perfect for: Glamorous evening attire that has a satin finish. Can be used in adorning jewelry or incorporated into intimate lingerie...

- **Jet Black:** With its connotations of mystery, elegance, and sophistication. It's the color of choice for those seeking to exude a seductive allure that is both Mysterious and powerful.

Perfect for: Perfect base color. To spice things up, add accents to your look in ruby red color.

- **White:** A color of heaven can also be incredibly sexy. Its brightness draws the eye, and when juxtaposed against the deeper skin tones, it can create a striking and enticing contrast.

Perfect for: It can be any piece of attire, be it casual or formal. It can be exquisitely paired with sophisticated tones of ruby red, emerald green, classic black, glittering gold, and sleek silver. These color combinations not only enhance the beauty of the garment but also contribute to an iconic, timeless look.

- **Silver:** Exudes a cool allure with its subtle shimmer and sophisticated palette. Its delicate luminescence whispers a promise of elegance and mystique, making it a stunningly seductive choice in fashion.

Perfect for: Sexy evening dress and accessories.

- **Gold:** A color often associated with luxury and extravagance, possesses an inherent seductiveness. Its rich hue captures the eye, imparting a sense of opulence reminiscent of radiant sunsets and gleaming treasures. It's a color that commands attention, making it an excellent choice for those wishing to make a striking, glamorous impression

Perfect for: luxurious event attire and accessories.

Pink: This tender and lively shade invokes a comforting, reminiscent feeling, transporting one back to the carefree days of youth. The symbolic meaning of love, romance, and even desire.

Perfect for: Beguiling summer dresses, alluring tops and sweaters, enticing accessories, and seductive nail art.

Midnight Blue: It Oozes sophistication and elegance, akin to a moonlit night sky. The deep hue of midnight blue cloaks you in an aura of intrigue and mystery. In the realm of color psychology, blue resonates with trustworthiness and reliability.

Perfect for: Formal evening wear will give the most power to the color, in every day this is not considered a seductive color.

Nude (according to your skin): Nude is a color that emanates warmth and comfort, invoking a tranquil and secure ambiance. When matched impeccably with your skin tone, this hue can yield a remarkable "Bare Skin" effect, which can be cleverly exploited for your agenda.

Perfect for: Day-to-day attire. A well-fitted cashmere dress in a nude tone, for example, can translate you into a ''Sex Appeal Goddess.''

Aphrodisiac Scents

An enchanting aroma, so rare, that makes hearts beat in a rhythm unaware.

The Seductive Symphony of Scents: Splurging on the priciest perfume isn't always the key to enchanting allure when it comes to seducing with the scent. Do realize, Gorgeous, that some fragrances carry a hidden aphrodisiac essence. Be keen on discerning these intoxicating notes in your perfume, or better yet, embark on a journey of crafting your very own bespoke scent that has something that represents you, just with a secret bonus on the side.

"You Know…She Knows" Aroma: Make your own love potion by handpicking essential oils and mixing them with your creams or base oils. In doing so, you're not simply cloaking yourself in a perfume—you're adorning yourself with your unique aromatic signature, an undeniable essence of "You," radiating an irresistible enchantment.

List

- **Ylang-Ylang:** This exotic, floral scent envelopes the senses, creating a mood-booster. And you know, a good mood leads to being flirty sometimes.

- **Sandalwood, Pheromone Mirror:** The scent of sandalwood, sweet, earthy, and woody, is not just pleasing but mirrors the human pheromone, androsterone, making it a natural aphrodisiac. Its fragrance relaxes the mind, reducing inhibitions and creating an atmosphere for mutual attraction.

- **Cinnamon:** The spicy, warm scent of cinnamon is a sensual invitation. It creates a home feeling. And that can instantly make you more appealing to anyone.

- **Vanilla:** The sweet, warm scent of vanilla is a potent aphrodisiac, evoking a sense of comfort and serenity. It wraps the senses in a cozy embrace, subtly stirring sentiments of attraction and desire. The scent of vanilla stirs a fervor, a certain pull that is hard to overlook and it particularly works within the male populace. This fragrance seems to amplify their sensual thirst more than other essences *in my personal experience*.

- **Lavender – The Soothing Aphrodisiac:** Lavender, renowned for its calming aroma, serves as a potent reliever of anxiety and stress, instilling a deep sense of relaxation. It triggers the brain's dopamine receptors responsible for pleasure and reward. This tranquil scent weaves a serene atmosphere, accentuating the intimacy and satisfaction inherent in romantic encounters.

- **Blood Orange – The Sensual Serenade:** The vibrant fruit indirectly stirs the pot of sensual desire by promoting relaxation and easing bodily tension. A serene mind and body fan the flames of passion, paving the way for a mesmerizing encounter.

- **Jasmine – The Universal Attractor Factor:** Jasmine, an ancient charmer, has long captivated us with its rich, sweet, and subtly musky aroma. Its intoxicating scent is known to kindle passion and foster intimacy across genders, harmoniously balancing sweet femininity with wild masculine undertones.

- **Saffron – The Warm and Spicy Temptress:** Saffron's warm, earthy fragrance with a hint of sweetness draws you into a tranquil space. Known as an aphrodisiac, it soothes the mind, alleviates anxiety, and fosters intimacy.

Potions

The Nostalgic Elixir: Known as pumpkin spice mix, this mesmerizing fusion of cinnamon, cloves, ginger, nutmeg, and allspice that compose the essence of pumpkin spice goes further than taste buds. It serves as a potent aphrodisiac, weaving a tapestry of allure that enfolds your chosen one in a comforting cocoon of warmth, evoking the nostalgic charm of home. This powerful sensory potion breathes depth into any rendezvous, morphing it into an instance of profound, soulful connection.

Paradise Garden: Jasmine, Tuberose and Ying-Yang, the floral seductress of our aphrodisiac ensemble. Their scents, exotic, intoxicating, and utterly irresistible, dance together to stir the senses and awaken untold desires. Perfect for any moment – a crisp morning, languid afternoon, or sultry evening – this medley whispers a sultry invitation to embark on a thrilling journey of sensory paradise garden feeling.

The Dance of Desire: Vanilla and Patchouli. Imagine the allure of sweet, soothing vanilla locking in a flirtatious tango with earthy, grounding patchouli. This playful duet is a potent love potion, awakening a dormant desire and sending ripples of pure anticipation through your senses. The comforting whispers of vanilla, combined with the provocative rawness of patchouli, create irresistibly enticing harmony. This enticing blend is a delicate yet powerful invitation to an unforgettable journey of sensory delight.

So come, my dear, don't hold back—embrace your elixir and let the world feel your enchanting presence.

How to Use The Essential Oils

Skin and Essential Oils – A Symphony: The topical application of essential oils paints a soothing aura around you. Dilute these oils with a carrier before applying them to the skin. Feel coated in the invisible allure.

Massage – The Aromatic Touch: Essential oils mixed in base oil, create a powerful touch. This potent combination serves as an aphrodisiac, spinning an intimate ambiance and maintaining that sensual energy.

Bathing – A Blissful Soak: Envision a bath sprinkled with essential oils, transforming your soak into a luxury. Just remember to avoid letting the scented bathwater touch your eyes, nose, or mouth.

Diffusing – A Roomful of Enchantment: A diffuser allows your chosen scent to pervade the room, an ideal choice for those who prefer the aroma without skin contact and a perfect choice for setting the mood in a designated area.

Word to Wise: It's important to remember that essential oils can cause skin burns if not properly diluted due to their high concentration. Additionally, they can trigger allergic reactions. Always ensure to use them responsibly and appropriately. Protect your eyes, ears, nose, mouth, and sensitive areas from direct application. If discomfort occurs, rinse immediately with warm, soapy water.

Feeling Sexy Rituals

"You Know...She Knows" Approved Guide

Ignite that alluring sexy spark that's just waiting to flicker within you.

Your Basics: Remember, your libido reflects your overall health and well-being. So that following rituals would really work you need to start taking care of your body, mind, and soul. This includes a healthy eating regimen (my personal preference is the Mediterranean diet), engaging in physical activities, and ensuring quality sleep. These three elements are the base layer.

Take Out the Garbage: Another important element that needs your attention, so that rituals would be effective is to embrace the art of letting go. Sometimes, the sexiest feeling is the liberating sensation of release. Whether it's an unfulfilling friendship, a limiting belief, or even letting go of your underwear for a night out. letting go can be incredibly empowering. By making the conscious choice to free yourself from what no longer serves you, allow a refreshing breeze of positivity to enter your life, or even between your legs.

Enhance: At times, specific behavioral patterns and actions can effectively enhance our feelings of sexiness. I'm confident that most of us can identify at least one such instance. Thus, I am eager to share my list with you. Feel free to utilize and expand upon it to suit your unique requirements and experiences.

Recipe

1. **The Main Character Walk:** Never underestimate the magnetic allure of an "All Shower" where you shave, exfoliate, and indulge in a fragrant hair mask. Feeling fresh and extra clean. followed by your favorite moisturizer, leaving you feeling irresistibly radiant. On top of it head out for your errands or meetings, wearing your favorite outfit and listening to your favorite music in headphones. Feeling like you are in music-video, the main character vibe.

2. **Tap into the Power of Sensual Home Dress:** Consider wearing something that makes you feel like a "Sexy Main Character" while doing everyday tasks - like making pancakes. It can be lace underwear adorned with roses, paired with comfortable beautiful silk pants, creating a tantalizing contrast of comfort and sensuality. Maybe it's an all-white ensemble featuring a transparent mesh bra under a white unbuttoned satin blouse, complete with matching white satin pants. Simply having a casual cup of coffee in sensual homeware can make your day extremely sexy, whether is it the combination I just mentioned or your personal choice of sexy-comfort attire.

3. **Sensual Yoga:** Great way to connect with your body and feel sexy in every cell, release stored emotions, and feel more in tune with your sexuality. You can practice it in the comfort of your own space or a fitness studio.

4. **Mirror Dance:** Put on music you enjoy, dim the lights, and watch yourself in the mirror while dancing, imagining that you are staring at your very own music video. Let the music guide your body letting your inhibitions go. Move gracefully, feeling the rhythm flowing through you. Sway

your hips, feeling the sensuality in every movement. Embrace your inner sexy star, and let yourself shine. Feel the joy and exhilaration that comes from expressing yourself through movement. Take this moment to celebrate your body, your sensuality, and your unique beauty. Dance to the beat of your own heart, and revel in the feeling of empowerment and freedom that this mirror dance brings. You deserve to feel confident, sexy, and amazing. Let the mirror be your reflective stage, and show the world (or rather, yourself) just how fabulous you truly are.

5. **Story Potion:** Writing down your sexual desires offers a platform for self-reflection and exploration. It can make desires seem more real and attainable, creating a sense of anticipation that can stimulate your libido. The more intricately you detail your scripts, the more vividly you can visualize these scenarios, and the more your sexual desire gets heightened. Bonus points if you Cultivate your sexual scripting into a lustful narrative, a personalized erotic story that can serve as a beautifully crafted "Libido Potion". You can read it before a night out, or before leaving for a date, to exude more libido. It can even help rekindle passion if you're in a long-term relationship where a "Friendly Routine" has taken place.

6. **Sexiness Layer:** What is that? It is a layer you put on top of an activity that you have mastered, and feel comfortable doing. It's about letting the "Sexy Self" out while doing your craft. Let's say you are a great cook, so cooking does not give you stress and you can top it off by feeling sexy and playful doing it. Imagine wearing a nice off-shoulder dress and winging your hips to music while you make that outstanding dinner you take pride in.

Bonus Hot Archetypes

Get Inspired!

The "Dark Femme"

Let's dive into the deep waters of dark femme.

Deep Start: Dark femme is not limited to a classic black gown with a smokey eye. It's a vibe that resonates with femininity and seduction by using sensuous allure. Embracing this look is a lifestyle choice, a commitment to embodying this captivating enigma aesthetic entirely. You know what they say: once a dark femme, always a dark femme.

Moon's Mystique: This style is a tantalizing tribute to the enigma that every woman holds within. We, as women, mirror the moon, dancing in rhythm with phases and natural cycles. The moon—a beacon of femininity, bathed in intrigue, embodies the promise of renewal and transformation. The "Dark" does not signify that she is evil but rather represents the depths, much like the moon's obscured side. This style is a flirtatious whisper of the secrets we keep, the allure we possess, and the captivating transitions we undergo. It's a testament to the power that comes from embracing the beautiful complexities of one's own personal darkness, akin to the mystery of the moon's unseen depths.

Ready to Leave a Mark: We've all heard the tales of those women who cross our paths and forever imprint themselves in our minds, the "Femme Fatales". This aesthetic can lead you to be one of them. When you embrace this aesthetic, you can discover an entirely new stream of feminine power within you.

Inside the Dark Femme: Her best trait is being unapologetically herself, embracing every part of herself. The shadowed femininity is marked by profound emotional resonance. Every emotion she honors. This is not a measure of negativity or positivity but rather a testament to the authentic depth and sincerity of these emotional expressions.

Sensuality: The shadowed femininity exudes a profound sensuality, deeply connected with her physical being and the surrounding universe. Every moment, every sensation is a feast to be savored. For her, sensuality transcends the mere physical realm—it's a thorough immersion, a reverent appreciation of life itself.

Empathy: Her femininity is imbued with deep-seated wisdom. If she had encountered suffering then it has fostered her an innate understanding of it, making her a wellspring of empathy. She wields her past not as a sword but as a lighthouse, guiding others through their tumultuous seas toward the tranquil shores of healing.

Protection: While her heart is full of kindness, the shadowed femininity also embodies a protective spirit. She maintains her position and guards her limits, ensuring the preservation of her integrity and the safety of those she holds dear. This balance between tender compassion and unwavering resilience forms the core of the dark feminine, a force that is both nurturing and formidable.

Envision This...

Notice Her: A woman makes her entrance into the coffee shop. It's a typical day, but she introduces an element of the extraordinary with her attire—a black silk dress. The hint of lace gracing her décolleté introduces an element of sex appeal that she does not shy away from, hinting at tales untold. Her hair is freely cascading down her shoulders. The centerpiece of this enigma is an antique pendant nestling against her collarbone, a silent storyteller whispering of history only she knows. Her calculated meanderings around the room have the room held in a vice-like grip, the power of her femininity undeniable and intoxicating. Long, feminine nails painted a deep burgundy, as rich as red wine, accentuate her every gesture. Her lips, accented with deep color lipliner, speak volumes even before they part, transforming her speech into a moving masterpiece. Every aspect of this woman sings a deeply personal sonnet of strong femininity.

Crafting the Vibe:

1. **Dress that Speaks:** Your wardrobe boasts of long, striking dresses and skin-tight ones adorned with turtlenecks, flare sleeves, and lace-up parts. Each piece is a testament to your hypnotic allure.

2. **Everyday Casual:** The black long silk skirt is your everyday Jeans. Wearing a lace-up corset is just as casual as sliding in your favorite sweater.

3. **Colors:** Opt for the boldness of bloody red, the mystery of deep violet, and the classic charm of black all weave an intoxicating narrative of dark beauty. Not to forget, midnight blue, since she is the queen of the mood.

4. **Accent Play:** Accent fabrics of choice—silk, satin, leather, velvet, mesh—each contributes to your unique blend of enchantment and power. Lace threads a delicate path through your outfits, adding just the right touch of femininity to your awe-inspiring ensemble. Imagine a long black see-through dress made out of lace flower-like lace, giving off a flirtatious tease as you move.

5. **The Enigma of Outerwear:** To embody the alluring ethos of the dark femme, opt for a dark trench coat. This piece of

outerwear is more than just clothing; it's a statement of mystery and allure. As you stand in the street awaiting your ride, cloaked in your trench coat, you become an irresistible force of intrigue and unattainability, a true femme fatale.

6. **Choose Footwear that Enthralls:** Opt for boots, dark as night, and made from suede and leather. Look for details that mesmerize: intricate lace-up patterns that hint at your captivating character. Step into these commanding heels and walk the path of allure and power.

Occasion: It's a lifestyle choice - **Once a dark femme always a dark femme.**

Red-Hot Details

The Vintage Bride's Seduction: Imagine an off-white lace dress – an embodiment of pure allure. Laced with vintage nuances and corset-like accents, it meticulously traces your body lines, regardless of the dress length. Complement it with fiercely bold, blood-red nails and lips to match, and you've morphed into a vintage bride aura, dripping with audacious sex appeal. This isn't just a look; it's as powerful as poison.

The Ultimate Seduction Game: There's no scream of allure louder than a patent leather trench coat. This glossy, black canvas draped over your shoulders effortlessly expresses a power that fuels your goddess-like aura. Long black boots add an intimidating yet enticing edge, and your hair, flowing behind you as you walk, becomes the dark river of mystique that draws everyone in. Now, for the pièce de résistance: the surprise that lies beneath. Imagine showing up at the door of your chosen one, the trench coat revealing nothing but a hint of lace underwear beneath. This unexpected move of seduction is more than just a statement; it's a memory carved into their mind, that will haunt their dreams forever.

The "Champagne Woman"

If you are ready to be visible, and bold, then let these curtains unfold the magic behind them!

Being Iconic: Exuding the essence of this aesthetic is about more than just visibility. It's about shining brilliantly, standing out, and owning the stage of life. You are not just playing the game; you are the game. Embodying the "Champagne Woman" means laying all your cards on the table, not out of desperation but from a position of strength. You are comfortable in your skin, flawlessly confident from head to toe, with nothing to hide and every reason to stand tall in your absolute perfection.

The Trophy Effect: The imprint you leave on others transcends mere beauty – it's akin to an unattainable prize. However, the power doesn't belong to the ones who admire you but to you who wield it. Be smart and keep that in mind. Bask in the rich rewards that this aesthetic brings you. Beauty and power aren't just intertwined, they are your tools to conquer, serving as the dual force you utilize to your advantage. You're not just a pretty facade, you're a power player in the grand game of life.

Envision This...

Resplendent Radiance: As she steps onto the grand expanse of the ballroom, she is a diamond set aglow. Draped in a champagne color dress that shimmers with each movement, an embodiment of celestial luminescence, she becomes the cynosure of all eyes. Her eyeshadow, harmonized effortlessly with her attire, enhances her captivating countenance. Her luminous Hollywood smile, as exquisite as pearls, blinds onlookers, leaving them entranced. She seems to have it all; this is the diamond of aesthetics. A compelling reflection of her vibrant personality is mirrored in her appearance, with a sense of luxury suffusing her every gesture. She is akin to the finest champagne—opulent, effervescent, and a connoisseur's delight, always ready to toast to the splendors of life, designed for the grandest of soirees.

Glamour Goddess: Her hair, each lock an embodiment of perfection, shimmers under the chandelier's light, brushed with a reflective balm that adds a layer of luster. Shimmer and sparkle seem to be the core elements of her being, reflected in the glittering eyeshadow and her diamond-studded accessories. Her lips, opulent and soft as a dew-kissed rose petal, glisten in the light. The luminous highlight that graces her cheeks mirrors the effusive sparkle of the world's most exquisite champagne.

The Aura of Grandeur: in her high heels, she matches the height of her ambitions and expectations of life. Her presence instills an inexplicable feeling of privilege in others. Those within her immediate orbit feel blessed, as though they've been touched by an angel. With her around, life appears more beautiful, more celebratory. It's her aura that infuses a sense of grandeur into the environment, making every moment an occasion worth celebrating.

Occasion: Whenever you feel like on top of the world, or that's just how you want to feel through your aesthetics. Remember: You must embody it fully if it's your chosen aesthetic. Own it!

Crafting the Vibe:

1. **The Dress that Dazzles:** For those nights that call for opulence and glamour, the choice of dress is paramount. Opt for hues that exude a Royal feeling. Envision dresses adorned with golden drapes, sparkling red to ignite hearts like fireworks, silver mini dress with an eye-catching diamond or Christal necklace, and a pristine white outfit complemented by chandelier earrings. The allure is in the extravagant glamour. Don't hesitate to pair these exquisite pieces with feather or faux fur coats for added drama. Because when it comes to making a grand entrance in a champagne goddess dress, there is truly no such thing as too much, as long as there is harmony in the choice of your colors.

2. **Iconic Fabrics:** When the call of the evening is seduction and allure, your choices of fabrics become a tantalizing game of visual appeal and tactile sensation. Starting with the feathers, it's an old glam staple, but this can add to a simple outfit the perfect amount of the extravaganza. Sequin fabric, sparkling under the lights, or fabrics adorned with crystals and pearls as your partners in this dance of decadence, transforming you into a vision that leaves an unforgettable impression.

3. **Champagne Afternoon:** Just because you're stepping out for a casual coffee to meet with friends doesn't mean you should compromise on your distinctive charm. Maintain a captivating vibe with choices like elongated silk skirts, blouses in champagne hues, or pristine white pantsuits. Not forgetting the allure of gold/silver accessories or crystals/diamonds that exude opulence and power. Make a statement in monochrome outfits that are the epitome of chic and sophistication. These staples don't just ensure you're dressed down in style, but they also ensure you're dressed with an air of effortless glamour—because when you're a

goddess of champagne, every day is an opportunity to sparkle.

4. **Champagne Feet:** Footwear is not just decorative additions but eloquent narrators of your fashion tale. Indulge in the perennial charm of shoes that intertwine ageless grace with a tantalizing twist. Picture a pair of golden strappy sandals or the lethal sophistication or stilettos with diamond tennis anklets. Those who favor a grand display dare to venture into the territory of thigh-high boots. Veer away from the cumbersome, grounding instead in slender and streamlined shapes. Shoes are the full stop in your fashion statement. Ensure they leave a point of exclamation.

Red-Hot Details

Next Level: Elevating the "Champagne Woman" aesthetic is no easy feat, yet there exists one mesmerizing path. Transform yourself into the Empress of a fantastical realm: Whether you borrow the ethereal grace of a Greek goddess or the arresting charm of a fantasy Empress, this is the ultimate way to elevate an already daring and distinctive look to the next level, giving it fantasy or royalty aura on top.

- **Music Industry Goddesses:** Usually this is used by most famous female singers in their concerts, they love to take champagne goddess into a vision of a fantasy empress while they're on stage.

The "Old Money Enchantress"

Let your style narrate an exquisite yet sprightly tale of seduction.

Envision this:

A Grand Entrance: As the clubhouse doors swing open, she makes her entrance. A vision in navy and white, she seems to have effortlessly plucked her ensemble straight from the pages of a luxury magazine. The rich navy of her tennis skirt crowned with a waistband that highlights her waist is an exquisite match to her tight-fit polo shirt, complemented with a "Super Round Bra" under, creating an hourglass-like body. This combination not only accentuates her figure but also exemplifies an understated elegance. Her raven-black hair, styled to what I call "Rich Girl Hair"[5] perfection, further emphasizes her exquisite features. Everywhere she goes, a subtle aura follows, making her the focal point of admiring glances and whispers of intrigue. She is... "The Old Money Enchantress." Taking her place by the window, she elegantly cradles her cup of tea as she raises the cup to her meticulously defined lips. Her timeless gold watch captures the light, highlighting her well-moisturized what looks like tennis player arms. She isn't just present in the moment; she's defining it.

Iconic Thinking: Imagine the allure you emanate, just like a clubhouse enchantress, radiating a palpable sense of seduction. You are no ordinary woman; you're a modern-day

---

[5] *"Rich girl hair"*: side-parted shoulder-length hair that has been curled and teased into voluminous perfection.

Charlotte York, fresh from your break with Trey and ready to command attention in every room you grace. Your determination is evident, and **you know your worth**. The transformation is absolute, and your wardrobe? Exquisite.

Occasion: Think of this ensemble as your style Swiss Army knife—infinitely adaptable for life's myriad moments. With the right mix-and-match, this look transcends boundaries, making it your go-to for virtually any setting. Wherever life takes you, from impromptu brunches to unexpected business meetings, this look won't just get you through the day; it'll make your day. Unlike others, this one will get you through a formal meeting with feminine charm and keep it classy, as long as you don't go all in.

Crafting the Vibe:

1. **Style Investment:** Strive for an enduring look that transcends fleeting fashion trends. Consider classic pieces and cuts that promise an ageless appeal, an investment into your style rather than a mere purchase.

2. **Sartorial Charm:** Your ensembles are classic pieces tailored to perfection, turtlenecks, palazzo pants, and cashmere dresses. Think "Old Money" standard clothing, just tailored so that lines of your body are showing. Perhaps you'll even surprise everyone with the sporty sophistication of a tennis-style dress. You wisely opt for a color palette that exudes timeless charm—the stalwart navy, the pristine white, the seductive black, the understated beige, and occasionally, the bold and captivating red.

3. **Reminder:** Don't hide under layers of clothing; if you opt for palazzo pants, then the top part of your body needs to

be tight or with a hint of skin, of course, if a tight fit makes you feel good.

4. **Hair Sophistication:** Your hair is the frame that brings your face into focus. Whether you let it cascade in gentle, perfectly done waves or pin it back into a graceful updo, it's always class all the way. Remember, hairstyle with an effort can elevate your entire look and give a sense of luxury aura around you.

5. **Accessorize Thoughtfully:** Consider accessories as an embodiment of enduring sophistication. Pearls, whether dangling from your ears or draped around your neck, imbue a sense of legacy and luxury. Gold bangles and a classic feminine watch subtly catch the light, adding just the right amount of sparkle. Classic gold stud earrings are your casual choice. Don't forget the iconic tennis necklace and bracelet. It's kinda even a must to own at least one of them.

6. **Country Club Cleavage:** The choice of your neckline should echo your unwavering standards, becoming a tantalizing tease of your persona. Cradle your charm in the graceful curve of a boat, square, or the timeless u or v cut neckline. Avoid any type of heavy push-up open cleavage.

7. **Elegance in Essence:** Beyond clothing and accessories, the "Old Money Enchantress" look is about an aura. It's the poise with which you hold yourself exuding confidence.

Red-Hot Details

- **The Allure of the Silk Scarf Choker:** The silk scarf choker is an accessory of tantalizing temptation, a dangerously seductive nod to classic style. Its bold sexiness, mingled with the sophistication of silk, hints at a daring yet calculated rebellion. Paired with an open-shoulder dress – hotter than the spiciest chili pepper.

- **The White Tennis Skirt Phenomenon:** Let's dive into the secret knowledge of the white tennis skirt – a sartorial choice that's subtly provocative. While it's not written in any fashion rulebook, any TikTok dweller who's ventured into the comment sections will confirm this phenomenon. The power of a white tennis skirt is undeniable, leaving suitors entranced and speechless.

- **Painting the Scene Red:** RED, the color of passion and boldness, is an invaluable tool to enhance the hotness quotient in the "Old Money Enchantress" aesthetic. Picture yourself in a tight-fitting, red turtleneck sweater, hair elegantly combed back, and lips glossed in a matching shade, creating a fiery combination that is irresistibly appealing. Finished with large round stud golden earrings. This look is not just a statement, it's a siren call.

The "Mediterranean Goddess"

Euro Mediterranean: Before we begin, I want to clarify that my aesthetic perspective is based on the European Mediterranean impression, as it is the region I am most familiar with.

The Ultimate Allure: Let's dive deeper into the mystique, shall we? Imagine your skin kissed by the warm Mediterranean sun, your hair being gently tousled by the soothing sea breeze. You're flaunting a floral print dress that dances with your hips with every move you make, embodying the sultry feeling of the Mediterranean. This isn't just a transformation, Darling. This is a rebirth. It's time to liberate your inner carefree goddess, let her bask in the allure of the Mediterranean vibe, and ascend to the realms of irresistible charm.

The Setting: Think of the tempting blue waters, green Andalusian mountains, and that irresistible Mediterranean sun. These women embody the very essence of their surroundings, casting a spell that's impossible to break. Their secret? Being in harmonious sync with the beauty that surrounds them, there is something unattainable and natural about them. Yet, even amidst this vibrant palette of blues and greens, one cannot ignore the rocky landscapes of Greece. They are primarily known for mirroring the beauty of the nature around them.

Memory Lane:

Turning Time Back to Mediterranean Days: five years spent in the breathtaking tranquility of

Mediterranean hotspots like Mallorca, Marbella, and Ibiza, with frequent escapes to the romantic landscapes of Italy and Greece. I became so intimately acquainted with the local aesthetics that I could mirror it effortlessly, absorbing the mesmerizing surroundings that have shaped so many women, including myself.

The First Drop of Mediterranean Blood: In the prime of my youth, my early twenties, destiny wove a charming tale. A newfound love held my hand and led me to this Eden. Freshly liberated from the academic world, I was just beginning to savor my newfound love and life in one of the most stunning Mediterranean destinations.

The Discovery: The initial year was an absorption phase, a break from the rigors of academia, simply lounging in quaint cafes during the day and soaking in the environment. Before I knew it, I was more captivated by the Mediterranean charm than I had anticipated. I found myself meticulously observing these Mediterranean queens. Whether they were locals or had a holiday home in the country, they knew how to look drop-dead gorgeous, reflecting the beauty of nature in their aesthetics.

The Transformation: It wasn't long before I began reflecting on this vibe in my wardrobe, embracing the freedom and femininity that the Mediterranean style exudes. The change of places during the five years gave me a clear look at the full picture and authentic niche characters each Mediterranean reflects on the aesthetics. From the classic elegance of Mallorca fashion to the daring cuts of Ibiza, this style holds an inimitable blend of natural charm and timeless appeal. Embracing this style feels as liberating as exploring the sprawling Andalusian mountains.

The Epiphany: What struck me the most through these years? The way these Mediterranean queens had me hanging on their every move as I mentally took notes on what makes them the epitome of effortless allure. And because I'm a firm believer in spreading love, I'm here to dish out all the insider tips on how to achieve your own Mediterranean goddess transformation.

Occasion: Ideal for savoring every sun-kissed moment, this look is your go-to for sultry summer days, whether you're lounging in a charming small-town getaway or enjoying an intimate dinner. With its blend of casual femininity, you can seamlessly transition from day to night. Leaving a trail of a natural seduction.

Crafting the Vibe:

7. **Hair Flair:** Whether it's short and sassy or long and luscious, just make sure there's a hint of that airy natural wave. Let your locks feel free and wild! Add some texture spray for that after-the-swim hairstyle.

8. **Floral Fantasy:** Opt for dainty floral prints or even classic polka dots. If there is a print, it's always playful and flirty.

9. **Curve Appeal:** Cinch it at the waist! Think cute corsets with delicate buttons or a snazzy belt to highlight those curves.

10. **Ready to Play:** The dress must have a playful character. Think of flirty hemlines that tease with every step. It's all about that playful aura that makes not just your outfit but also you utterly irresistible.

11. **Feels like Heaven:** Choose flowy and breathable fabrics that feel dreamy against the skin. Think cotton or linen for that light and natural feeling.

12. **Daring Decollate:** Flaunt that neckline and those shoulders. A hint of skin can add that extra oomph to your Mediterranean goddess vibe. But remember, always have it glowing, though.

13. **Rustic Accessories:** The embodiment of the Mediterranean aesthetic is not complete without the mesmerizing allure of bewitching accessories. Consider delicate layered necklaces cascading down your neckline or a pair of sultry hoop earrings swaying with every movement. Remember, it's all about adding that hint of rustic charm with a dash of sophistication.

14. **Flirty Feet:** Adorning your feet is all about infusing a hint of lively allure. Choose lace-up sandals, venture into vibrant color palettes, and think about accentuating with anklets for an added sprinkle of flirtatious charm. For heels, consider embellishments such as roses or flowers to further enhance their visual appeal.

Red-Hot Details

- **Bold Goddess:** Red nails and a white dress. Picture this: you in a pristine white dress, the angelic being. But wait, what's that? Your red nails boldly announce that there's more to you than meets the eye. Yes, Darling, you're a paradox, and you're loving it.

- **The Subtle Seductress:** Blushed Décolleté mixed with off-shoulder dress. A hint of blush graces your décolleté, making you look sensuous like you have spent a day at the beach. It's the cherry on top of your irresistible ensemble.

- **Corseted dress with breast-holding cups:** The corset cinches in your waist while the strategically placed cups uplift and pop out your "Girls." This exceptional body-sculpting garment ensures a stunning silhouette that will undoubtedly captivate and enchant onlookers.

- **The Tender Temptress:** Delicate Lover Belly Chain. This isn't just an accessory; it's a statement. It gracefully traces the curve where your waist meets your hips, beckoning the eye to a place of flirtatious allure. Honey, you're not just adorning your body; you're making it a magnetic field that looks impossible to resist.

So, are you ready to soak in the Mediterranean sun, even if it's just metaphorically? Dive in, Darling. Your ultimate glow-up awaits!

Bonus Cheat Sheet

For Seductive Style Combinations

The Smart Seductress: Now, Gorgeous, bear in mind that any game has its rules. The secret game, when playing with garments, is all about spinning an irresistible charm that leaves them desiring more. It's about providing a subtle preview of your charms, thereby igniting the spectator's imagination to craft their sensual narrative, eager to know where the story unfolds.

Stay True to Yourself: Imagine yourself as a half-painted work of art, awaiting the final touches that will bring it to complete fruition. Review the following options carefully and cherry-pick those that resonate most with you.

Cheat Sheet

- **The Allure of an Open-back Dress:** It's an unexpected revelation, a tantalizing glimpse into the forbidden. The demure front gives way to an audacious back, creating a thrilling contrast that stirs the imagination.

- **The Allure of a Mini Skirt Paired With Long Socks:** This ensemble exudes a tantalizing dichotomy—a playful nod to youthfulness coupled with a covert sensuality. This juxtaposition of innocence and seduction.

- **Visible Nipples Through Soft Fabric Dress:** Fell like a Goddess of the paradise garden, subtly showcasing the outline of your nipples is an intoxicating statement of sensual allure. This bold revelation of the body triggers the imagination and stirs deep-rooted instincts.

- **A Red Silk Slip Dress With Stiletto Heels:** The silky smooth fabric and the sensual red hue is a potent combination of mystery and seduction, amplified by the daring stilettos.

- **The Timeless Little Black Dress Paired with Thigh-high Boots:** This classic ensemble oozes seduction, with the boots adding a provocative edge to the elegant dress.

- **A Sheer White Blouse with a Black Lace Bralette Underneath, Paired with a High-waisted Pencil Skirt:** The chic contrast of colors and the tantalizing glimpse of the bralette through the sheer fabric is an erotic fantasy of an office environment.

- **Sensuous Lace Bodysuit with Deep V cut, paired with a Structured Black Blazer:** The intricate lace bodysuit invites the observer into an intoxicating realm of fantasy, stirring notions of intimate encounters. Simultaneously, the structured black blazer bestows upon the wearer an aura of authority and control. This sophisticated juxtaposition elevates the ensemble to a captivating narrative of dominance and flirtiness, empowering you while enthralling those onlookers.

- **Super Long Dress With an Almost Full-length Slit on the leg:** The sweeping length of the dress whispers of regal sophistication, while the daring cut reveals a seductive glimpse of the leg, creating a thrilling interplay of modesty and daring reveal. This dress toys with the observer's imagination as it oscillates between covering and uncovering with each step you take. The interplay of mystery and reveal, coupled with the graceful movement of the fabric as it swirls around the leg, adds an intoxicating element of seduction to this outfit.

- **Trench Coat Surprise:** Imagine showing up at the door of your chosen one wearing a trench coat. Wearing nothing but lace lingerie with suspender. This unexpected move of seduction is more than just a statement; it's a memory carved into their mind, a hypnotic allure that will haunt their dreams forever.

- **Off-shoulder Sweater With Long Earrings and Hair Pinned Up:** This ensemble paints a tantalizing image of you being naked and draped in nothing but a soft, enveloping blanket while the earrings cascade in a captivating display. It subtly enhances the neck and shoulders, offering a mere hint of nudity—a provocative tableau left for the imagination to complete.

- **The White Tennis Skirt Phenomenon:** Let's dive into the secret knowledge of the white tennis skirt—a sartorial choice that's subtly provocative. While it's not written in any fashion rulebook, any TikTok dweller who's ventured into the comment sections will confirm this phenomenon. The power of a white tennis skirt is undeniable, leaving suitors speechless.

Final Thoughts

My beautiful Reader, mastery of allure isn't simply about having the Coke bottle figure or the sharpest cheekbones. It's about the woman who walks into a room and, without uttering a single word, makes a statement. She's so finely attuned to her essence that she's turned it into an art form, an enchanting symphony that leaves everyone in awe.

A woman who captivates, who knows her angles and has mastered her style to the extent that it becomes an extension of her very being. It's not just about donning a killer outfit; it's about crafting an entire "**You Know...She Knows**" aura around you that says, "Yes, I'm here, and yes, you want to know my story. "

Everyone wants to look like they've just stepped out of a Vogue editorial shoot. But what if you could live that editorial every single day? That's right. Everyday moments can be made extraordinary. Your life doesn't have to be a series of mundane routines. Rather, it can be a runway show where you are both the star and the creative director, and repeating effort always surpasses those who ride just what's given to them by nature.

The unspoken power of a well-curated look, a flash of bewitching eye contact, a swish of a perfectly styled mane—these are your secret weapons. And the best part? This power resides in all of us. From the "Champagne Woman" of Dubai to the boho-chic goddesses of Ibiza, every woman can unlock her unique form of magnetism. Trust me; I've seen it firsthand, from catwalks to exotic locales, and the transformative power of mastering your allure is universal.

So, for everyone who's daring to venture on this journey of magnetic self-discovery, to all those who're ready to turn everyday moments into photo-worthy memories, this is your moment. Unleash your inner siren and let her sing. You're not just owning your look; you're owning your life.

My aspiration is that this book has provided you with valuable insights to navigate your **sexy side** of life. Perhaps, you might already be anticipating a sequel - indeed, a second part could already be under development.

Keep it magically sexy. I'll be here whenever you need me again. Gorgeous, you've got this!

Love, always – @queen.vee.bee

Made in the USA
Las Vegas, NV
03 May 2024

89480010R10095